# National Parks: The Most Beautiful Islands

## *Most Enchanting Islands of the World*

**Keenah Lottie**

# Table of Contents

# Introduction

Traveling is one of the most enriching experiences we can have in life. When we venture out to explore new places, cultures, and traditions, we broaden our horizons and learn more about ourselves and the world around us.

Traveling allows us to discover the beauty and diversity of our planet and invites us to open our minds and hearts to the unknown. By experiencing new ways of life and different perspectives, we can come to better understand the complexity and richness of humanity.

In addition, it allows us to disconnect from our daily routine, get out of our comfort zone, and live unforgettable moments that will always be with us. It challenges us to overcome obstacles, learn new skills, and find creative solutions to unforeseen situations.

It's an adventure that enriches, transforms, and makes us grow as human beings. So if you get the chance, don't hesitate to hit the road and explore the world!

The islands are magical places, where nature seems to have taken pains to create true earthly paradises. Surrounded by the vast ocean, the islands are home to spectacular natural treasures found nowhere else in the world. From its white sand beaches and crystal clear waters to its exotic tropical jungles and spectacular cliffs, every corner of the island is an invitation to adventure and exploration.

But the islands aren't just nature lovers' dream spots, they're also home to fascinating cultures that have evolved over centuries without making contact with the rest of the world. Each island has its own history, traditions, and customs that can surprise and inspire visitors.

Island tourism is a once-in-a-lifetime experience, as it allows you to immerse yourself in a broad, complex, and diverse experience. Each island has its own flavor, sound, and aroma, which mixes in a symphony of unforgettable sensations. From trying exotic and authentic local cuisine to listening to traditional music passed down from generation to generation, island tourism is an invitation to experience the culture of a place authentically and excitingly. Well, the islands are a gift of nature that invites us to explore, learn and connect with ourselves and with the world around us.

In addition, island tourism can be an opportunity to contribute to the conservation of these unique ecosystems and the cultures that inhabit them. By choosing responsible and environmentally friendly tour operators, we can ensure that our visits to these islands do not negatively affect their delicate ecological and cultural balance.

This book is a tribute to the brave explorers who yearn to visit an island during their next vacation. In these pages, you will discover a specialized guide that will take you to discover the ten most wonderful islands in the world, all of them designated as national parks. Each of them has its own essence and offers a variety of natural landscapes that perfectly balance beauty and fun.

From white sand beaches to spectacular rock formations, through dense forests, and rich biodiversities, these islands are a gift for the senses. The balance between nature and recreation is one of the main attractions of these destinations, and this guide will show you how to get the most out of your experience.

If you're an intrepid traveler looking for a memorable experience, look no further than this guide to the world's ten most amazing islands. I promise you won't be disappointed and will take you to places you didn't even know existed.

There is something magical about an island vacation that cannot be found anywhere else. Just being surrounded by the sea, cool breezes, and natural beauty is enough to make you feel free and rejuvenated. The worries of the world melt away, stress melts away, and you feel at peace.

But the islands offer much more than just a relaxing getaway. You can enjoy a wide variety of water sports, from diving and snorkeling to surfing and kayaking. And there's nothing like watching the moonlit sky while walking on the beach or enjoying a sunset party.

But exploring an island not only gives you a chance to unwind, but it can also teach you a lot about nature and human impact on the environment. From observing marine life and coastal ecosystems to the effects of climate change on natural landscapes, each island offers a valuable lesson.

And last but not least, exploring an island can be a life-changing adventure. It takes you to places you've never seen before, introduces you to new cultures and people, and teaches you to appreciate the wonders of the world in a whole new way.

Welcome to this guide on island tourism in the most paradisiacal and exotic islands-national parks in the world. Here you will find detailed information about the different islands, their location, history, culture, climate, ecological value, human value, and wildlife. We will tell you how each of these islands has influenced the development of humanity, how they have evolved over the years, and how they are essential for the ecology and balance of the world's ecosystem. In addition, we will provide you with a complete list of activities that you can do in each destination to make your adventure unforgettable.

In addition, in this book, you will find information about the rich and varied gastronomy that each island has to offer. From fresh fish and shellfish to exotic fruits, you can sample a wide variety of flavors and textures. But not only that, we will tell you how each island has developed its own gastronomic identity over the years, and how the local cuisine reflects the history, culture, and traditions of the island.

But what is it that *really* makes these islands so special? It is its majestic natural beauty and the wide variety of outdoor activities that you can do. From hiking through lush tropical forests to snorkeling over coral reefs, each island has something unique and exciting to offer.

However, you must take precautions before visiting each destination. We'll provide you with detailed information on travel requirements, as well as some helpful tips to get the most out of your experience.

Join me on this quest to explore some of the most impressive and fascinating island-national parks in the world. Discover spectacular landscapes, unique biodiversity, and cultural treasures that will take your breath away. From the white sand beaches and crystal clear waters of the Caribbean to the coral reefs of the Bahamas, each island has something special and exciting to offer.

This adventure is just beginning.

# Chapter 1: Curaçao Islands

The Curaçao Islands are a true paradise for lovers of tropical beaches and underwater landscapes. With turquoise waters and white sands, it's easy to fall in love with its natural beauty. Every year, around 1 million tourists visit the island to enjoy its natural wonders and rich culture (Curaçao Tourist Board, 2021).

In the chapter of the book dedicated to this jewel of the Caribbean, its fascinating history, its vibrant culture, and its amazing biodiversity are explored in detail.

As the American poet and essayist Ralph Waldo Emerson said, "The beauty of the world is the wonder of each one of us" (1903).

## Location

The Curaçao Islands are located in the southern Caribbean Sea, about 64 kilometers (40 miles) north of the coast of Venezuela. It is part of the Lesser Antilles and is part of the Netherlands Antilles archipelago. Curaçao is the largest island in the archipelago and is located about 70 kilometers (43.5 miles) east of the island of Aruba and about 40 kilometers (25 miles) west of the island of Bonaire (Britannica, n.d.).

Although Curaçao is in a tropical zone, its location at the southern tip of the Caribbean protects it from hurricanes, so visitors can enjoy warm, sunny weather year-round. In addition, its strategic position makes it an important transit point for ships sailing to the Panama Canal and South America. With its stunning natural beauty and its rich history and culture, Curaçao is undoubtedly a premier tourist destination in the Caribbean.

## Short History

The main island of Curaçao is the third largest island in the Caribbean and its relief is mainly flat, although there are some low-lying hills and mountains. The geology of the island is characterized by its sedimentary and coral origin. The island was formed from sand and clay sediments deposited during the Cretaceous period, approximately 65 million years ago, which consolidated and uplifted as tectonic changes occurred. In addition, the coral reefs have also had a great influence on the formation of the island, since they developed over a long period of time, approximately 25 million years. Therefore, the island is composed mainly of sedimentary and coral rocks, which gives the island its characteristic white and rocky appearance (Calleja, C. W., & De Lisle, H, 2010).

The first inhabitants of the island were the indigenous Arawak, who arrived on Curaçao around 6,000 years ago. Subsequently, the caiques settled on the island around the year 1000 AD. In the 15th century, the Spanish arrived on the island and claimed it for the Spanish Crown. In 1634, the Dutch invaded the island and took it over. Curaçao became a major commercial and transportation center in the Caribbean, and the Dutch established a colony there (De La Fuente, S., 2010).

During the 17th and 18th centuries, the island experienced rapid economic growth thanks to the slave trade and sugar production. In 1863, the slaves were freed and Curaçao became a more liberal and democratic colony. In 1954, the Netherlands Antilles, including Curaçao, became autonomous territories within the Kingdom of the Netherlands (Koster, H.,1999).

In 2010, Curaçao became a self-governing country within the Kingdom of the Netherlands. Today, it is a country with its own constitution, government, and judicial system. Curaçao's form of government is a parliamentary monarchy, where the monarch is the King of the Netherlands and the head of government is the prime minister. Additionally, Curaçao has a multi-party political system, where political parties compete in free and fair elections (Paiewonsky, M., 1998).

# Culture and Language

The original inhabitants of the island of Curaçao were the Arawak, an indigenous tribe that lived there for centuries before the arrival of the Europeans. Currently, the native population of Curaçao is primarily of African, European, and Amerindian descent. The official language of Curaçao is Dutch. However, the majority of the population speaks Papiamento, a creole language that combines elements of Spanish, Portuguese, Dutch, English, and African languages. Additionally, English and Spanish are commonly spoken on the island, and many Curaçaoans are multilingual.

Music is an important part of Curaçao's culture, and the island is known for its Caribbean music, including the *tumba, waltz, merengue,* and *tambú*. The tambú is a type of music and dance native to the island, which was developed by African slaves as a way of expressing their culture and resistance (Koster, H., 1999).

Curaçao's gastronomy also reflects the influence of African, European, and Amerindian cultures. Typical island dishes include fresh fish, rice and beans, fried plantains, fish soups, and stewed kid. Furthermore, the island is known for its Curaçao liqueur, which is made from the Curaçao oranges, which grow on the island.

Curaçao is also known for its colorful houses in the Dutch colonial style, which are located in Willemstad, the capital of the island. The island's architecture has been influenced by Spanish, Portuguese, Dutch, and African cultures, giving Curaçao a unique and diverse feel.

Curaçao has a rich and diverse culture that is reflected in its festive and religious practices (Visit Curaçao, n.d.). One of the most important and popular festivities on the island is Carnival, which takes place in February and is a celebration of life, freedom, and the culture of Curaçao. During Carnival, costume parades, dances, and music take place in the streets.

Another important holiday is Dia di Bandera, which falls on July 2 and is a celebration of the island's identity and sovereignty. Parades, dances, music, and traditional foods are enjoyed.

Holy Week is also an important religious celebration in Curaçao, which includes processions, masses, and other religious events throughout the island. The Corpus Christi festival is also celebrated in Curaçao and other

Catholic countries and is an occasion to honor the presence of Jesus in the Eucharist.

Finally, the Festival di Tumba is a music festival that takes place in Curaçao before Carnival. This festival celebrates the traditional music of the island and brings together musicians and dancers from all over the region.

Festive and religious practices on Curaçao reflect the island's cultural diversity and are a source of pride and celebration for the island's inhabitants.

# Weather and Climate

The island has a hot and dry climate throughout the year, with average temperatures of 27 °C. The rainy season runs from October to January, but in general, the island receives very little precipitation.

Due to its location on the fringe of the Caribbean, the island does not really have defined seasons, but rather has a temperate and tropical temperature throughout the year. However, the year can be divided into two periods: a dry period from January to September, and a rainy period from October to December.

During the dry period, relative humidity is low, averaging 60%, and temperatures are warm and stable. During the rainy season, temperatures are slightly lower, but relative humidity is high, averaging 85%. Although the rains can be heavy at times during this period, the island generally receives little annual precipitation, averaging 550mm.

It is important to mention that although the island is not in the path of the hurricanes that affect the Caribbean during the hurricane season, which runs from June to November, it is possible to experience torrential rains and electrical storms due to nearby weather systems (World Weather Online, n.d.).

The ecological situation of Curaçao is interesting due to the presence of a large number of endemic species. The island has 187 plant species, of which

28 are endemic. There are also several endemic animal species, including several species of lizards and a snake, the Curaçaoan Rattlesnake.

However, the island also faces several environmental challenges, including coral reef degradation due to climate change and human activity, loss of natural habitats due to tourism development, and water and air pollution due to industrial activity and maritime navigation (IUCN, 2019; World Wildlife Foundation, n.d.).

To address these problems, Curaçao has implemented a series of policies and programs to protect the environment, including the creation of nature reserves and the promotion of eco-tourism. In addition, the island is working on the transition towards a more sustainable economy, through the development of renewable energy sources and the promotion of sustainable agricultural practices (Sociaal-Economische Raad, 2014).

# Tourist Attractions in Curaçao

Curaçao has a wide variety of impressive landscapes. From white sand beaches to rugged hills and cliffs, the island has something for everyone. If you are a nature lover, you cannot miss the Christoffel National Park (Curaçao Tourist Board, 2021). Located on the north end of the island, this park offers a variety of trails for walking and biking. Here you will find an abundance of native flora and fauna, including cacti and tropical birds. If you like nature, you can go hiking on one of the marked trails, such as the Christoffel Mountain trail, the Boka Grandi trail, or the Seru Bientu trail. The panoramic view from the top of the mountain is impressive.

The capital of Curaçao is Willemstad, a city full of colorful Dutch-style buildings. Stroll through the historic center, a UNESCO World Heritage Site, and admire the houses painted in blue, green, pink, and yellow. The view from the floating bridge over the bay of Santa Ana is spectacular.

Curaçao has a wide variety of beaches with crystal clear waters and white sand. Among the most famous are Playa Grote Knip, Playa Cas Abao, and Playa Porto Mari, all of which are ideal for snorkeling and scuba diving. If you're looking for a quieter beach, check out Daaibooi Beach (Curaçao

Tourist Board, 2021). With its white sand and crystal clear waters, Playa Grote Knip is the perfect place to relax and enjoy a day of sun and sea. If you prefer a livelier atmosphere, Mambo Beach is an excellent option. This beach has a wide variety of bars and restaurants and is very popular with tourists (Curaçao Tourist Board, 2021).

Curaçao has a rich history that goes back hundreds of years. As a result, the island has a wide variety of fascinating museums that will allow you to learn more about its cultural heritage. One of the most interesting museums is the Kura Hulanda Museum. Housed in a series of restored historic buildings in downtown Willemstad, this museum tells the story of the slave trade in the region. Inside, the history of slavery in the Caribbean and the African slave trade to America is exhibited. The exhibition features historical objects, paintings, and photographs.

Another impressive museum is the Maritime Museum. This museum has a large number of maritime artifacts, including ship models, navigational instruments, and fishing equipment. In addition, the museum also has an exhibition dedicated to the history of the Royal Navy of Curaçao.

Curaçao's rich history dates back to the time of the island's first inhabitants. As a result, there are many historical places worth visiting. One of the most impressive is Fort Amsterdam. Built in the 17th century to protect the island from invaders, this fort has been restored and is now a museum. From here, you can enjoy stunning views of the port of Willemstad (Curaçao Tourist Board, 2021).

The Curaçao Marine Aquarium is one of the most popular attractions on the island. In it, you can observe more than 400 marine species of the Caribbean in their natural habitat. In addition, boat trips and guided tours are offered.

Another historical place worth visiting is the Mikvé Israel-Emanuel Synagogue. Built in the year 1732, this synagogue is the oldest in continuous use in the Western Hemisphere. Here you can learn about the history of the Jewish community of Curaçao and their contribution to the island (Curaçao Tourist Board, 2021).

When it comes to Curaçao's nightlife, the island offers a wide variety of options for after-sunset fun. In addition to the many restaurants and bars found in Willemstad, the city also has discos and nightclubs where you can dance until the wee hours of the morning. The Pietermaai district is particularly famous for its bars and pubs with live music and a bohemian atmosphere.

It is also possible to enjoy traditional music and dance performances in Curaçao, such as the tambú, a style of African music and dance that originated in the days of slavery. There are several places on the island where you can see these shows live.

On the other hand, if you prefer a quieter atmosphere, you can opt for a night walk through the historic center of Willemstad, where the colorful houses and night lighting create a unique atmosphere. It is also possible to have a romantic dinner in one of the restaurants overlooking the sea and enjoy the cool Caribbean breeze.

# Accommodation

First of all, it is important to note that Curaçao has a wide variety of accommodations for all tastes and budgets. From luxurious resorts to modest hostels and apartments, the island has options for all travelers.

As for the best-rated hotels in Curaçao, most are located in the Willemstad area, the capital of the island. Some of the most prominent are:

- **Baoase Luxury Resort**: This five-star resort is one of the most luxurious in Curaçao. Located on a private beach, it has private villas with a pool, spa, and haute cuisine restaurant.

- **Santa Barbara Beach & Golf Resort**: Located on the east coast of the island, this five-star resort is known for its 18-hole golf course and its impressive views of the sea. It offers a wide range of rooms and suites, as well as activities such as water sports, boating, and diving.

- **Avila Beach Hotel**: This four-star hotel is located in the center of Willemstad and has a privileged location facing the sea. With more than 60 years of history, the Avila Beach Hotel is one of the most emblematic accommodations in Curaçao.

On the other hand, if you are looking for more modest and affordable accommodations in Curaçao, there are also several options available. Some of the most popular hostels and apartments are:

- **Happy Turtle Apartments**: These simple but cozy apartments are located in the quiet town of Westpunt, on the west end of the island. Each apartment has a kitchenette and a private terrace with sea views.

- **Piscadera Seaview Apartments**: These sea-view apartments are located in the Piscadera area, just a few minutes from Willemstad. They have an outdoor pool and a full kitchen in each apartment.

- **Hostels**: This is a popular option for travelers on a budget. They offer basic and cheap accommodation in shared or private rooms. Some of the most popular Curaçao hostels include The Ritz Village Hotel, Poppy Hostel, and City Hostel Curaçao. These hostels offer clean, simple rooms, shared bathrooms, and common areas for socializing. Prices range from $20 to $50 per night depending on season and location.

- **Camping**: This is an option for those looking for a more adventurous experience in Curaçao. Campgrounds allow travelers to enjoy nature and save money on lodging. Some of the most popular campsites on Curaçao are Campismo Eco-Logico, Cas Abao Resort, and Jan Kok Lodges. These campgrounds offer camping areas, basic facilities, and access to the beach and other outdoor activities. Prices range from $10-$20 per night depending on season and location. You can check their websites for more information.

As you can see, this wonderful island has a wide variety of accommodations for all tastes and budgets. From luxurious resorts to modest hostels and apartments, there are options for all travelers. The best-rated hotels are found mainly in the Willemstad area, with the best rooms offering stunning sea views, while the more modest accommodations are found in other parts of the island, further from the coast.

# Souvenirs Worth Buying

If you're looking for the best gifts and souvenirs to take home from your Curaçao vacation, you've come to the right place. The island is known for its diverse and vibrant culture, which means there are many unique options for shopping. Here are some of the best options to take as a souvenir of your trip:

- Curaçao liqueur: It is an alcoholic beverage made from the peel of the Curaçao orange. It is one of the most famous products on the island and is available in several flavors. You can buy a bottle as a souvenir or even a tasting set to try the different flavors.

- Hand-carved wooden items: Local artists in Curaçao are known for their wood carving skills. From carnival masks to animal figures, there are plenty of options to choose from. These wooden items are one of a kind and capture the essence of the island's culture.

- Larimar jewelry: Larimar is a semi-precious stone found exclusively in the Dominican Republic and the neighboring island of Saint Martin. However, jewelers in Curaçao also work with the stone to create beautiful pieces of jewelry. The shades of blue and green in the stone represent the sea and sky, making it a popular choice for a special keepsake.

- African culture items: As you know, Curaçao has a rich African heritage, and visitors can find many items representing this culture in the island's markets and souvenir shops. Some popular options include tribal masks, drums, and wooden sculptures.

- Aloe Vera products: The aloe vera plant is abundant on the island, and visitors can find many beauty and skin care products made with aloe vera. From moisturizers to shampoos to body washes, there are plenty of options to choose from.

- T-shirts and caps: Curaçao t-shirts and hats are an easy and affordable way to carry a souvenir of your vacation. You can find T-shirts with colorful designs that represent the island, as well as baseball caps with the Curaçao logo.

- Local sweets and chocolates: This island is famous for its local sweets and chocolates, which are unique in taste and design. Visitors can find confections made with local flavors such as coconut and mango, as well as chocolates with fruit and liqueur fillings.

- Local art: Curaçao's art community is very active and visitors can find many galleries and shops selling local art. From paintings and sculptures to photography and artifacts, there are many options to choose from.

# Discovering Delicacies

Due to the mixture of different roots, the cuisine of this island is rich in flavors, textures, aromas, and sensations. Here is a list of the best typical dishes and foods that you should not miss if you visit Curaçao:

- Keshi Yena: This is a traditional Curaçao dish that is made with a cheese topping and a filling of minced meat, olives, raisins, onion, and tomato. The mixture is simmered until the cheese melts and the filling is cooked.

- Sopa di pisca: It is a fish soup that is prepared with fresh fish, potatoes, sweet potato, celery, pepper, and coriander. It is served hot and is perfect for cold days.

- Arepa di pampuna: It is a kind of fried pancake made of pumpkin and corn, it is served as an accompaniment to some dishes or as a snack.

- Stobá: It is a meat stew made with beef or goat, onion, garlic, tomato, pepper, and coriander. It is served with rice and beans.

- Funchi: It is a typical dish made with cornmeal, water, and salt. It is a perfect accompaniment to stews.

- Ayaca: It is a cake made with cornmeal dough stuffed with pork, beef and chicken, olives, raisins, peppers, and onion. It is wrapped in banana leaves and steamed.

- Pastechi: It is a kind of empanada filled with minced meat, chicken, cheese, ham, or fish. It can be found in many places on the island, even on the streets.

- Pan Bati: It is a flatbread made with wheat flour, salt, sugar, and water. It can be eaten as a side dish or as a base for a sandwich.

- Kas di Yambo: It is a stew of pork liver, onion, garlic, tomato, and pepper. It is a popular dish in local restaurants.

- Yuana: It is a dish made with iguana, the meat is cooked with onion, garlic, tomato, pepper, and cilantro. It is served with rice and beans.

# 10 Advice Before Visiting Curaçao

This spectacular Caribbean island has a lot to offer tourists, but you must take certain precautions into account before visiting it. I have researched and compiled information from several reliable sources to offer you the top 10 precautions you should take before visiting this beautiful Caribbean island:

1. You should keep in mind that Curaçao is a very sunny island, so it is essential to bring sunscreen and use it throughout the day. In addition, you should wear light and comfortable clothing, since the climate is hot and humid throughout the year.

2. It is important to know that the official currency of Curaçao is the Netherlands Antillean guilder, although most places accept US dollars. However, it is recommended that you exchange some money for guilders for small purchases and expenses. Always have a little cash with you, as many street food and craft stalls do not accept other means of payment.

3. It is recommended that you find out about the entry requirements for Curaçao before you travel. Depending on your nationality, you may need a visa or tourist card to enter the country. You can find this information on the Curaçao government website.

4. If you intend to drive in Curaçao, you should know that it drives on the right and that you will need an international driving permit to rent a car. You should also keep in mind that the roads can be narrow and you should drive carefully.

5. You must inform yourself about the laws and regulations of the island before you travel. For example, smoking is prohibited in public places—as is the consumption of alcoholic beverages—and in most indoor establishments, and the use of marijuana is also prohibited.

6. You should know that electricity in Curaçao is 110 volts and that type A and B plugs are used. If your electrical devices use a different voltage, you will need an adapter.

7. It is recommended that you purchase travel insurance before traveling to Curaçao. This will protect you in case of illness, accident, or loss of luggage.

8. You should be aware that the island has a large number of beautiful beaches, but some of them can be dangerous due to currents. You must always follow the indications and safety regulations of the beach. If you are on a remote beach without lifeguard supervision, avoid swimming. Keep in mind that in addition to the currents, the local fauna may pose a threat to you, as your presence may in turn threaten their ecosystem.

9. You must respect the culture and traditions of the island. Curaçao is a multicultural island with a rich history and a unique mix of African, European, and Latin American influences. Learning about local culture and traditions can make your trip even more enriching.

10. Find out about the activities and events that take place on the island during your visit. Curaçao has a rich cultural life with festivals, concerts, and sporting events throughout the year. Be sure to check the events calendar before your trip so you don't miss out on any exciting activities during your stay. You can also check with the local tourist office for up-to-date information on events and activities on the island.

# Chapter 2: The Bahamas

The Bahamas is an archipelago located in the Atlantic Ocean that offers unparalleled natural and mystical beauty. Its beaches with crystal clear waters and white sands, together with its impressive coral reefs and exotic species of plants and animals, make this place a jewel of nature. The diversity of the marine fauna is astounding, with sharks, rays, sea turtles, and an abundance of colorful fish, while on land we find iguanas, pink flamingos, and tropical birds that adorn the local flora. The Bahamas is a world-class tourist destination noted for its unique and spectacular beauty.

The American poet Langston Hughes perfectly described the beauty of the Bahamas in his poetic work Bahamas Faith (1997) with the following lines:

"Oh, the Bahamas are beautiful,

the pale blue sea

and the sand white as snow

that stretches for miles."

## Location

The Bahamas is an archipelago located in the Atlantic Ocean, southeast of Florida, United States, and northeast of Cuba and the island of Hispaniola. The approximate geographic coordinates are 24 degrees north latitude and 76 degrees west longitude. The archipelago consists of more than 700 islands and cays, only a few of which are inhabited.

The archipelago is located in the region known as the West Indies, within the area known as the Antilles. The island chain extends for about 1,000 kilometers (620 miles) in a southeast-northwest direction, covering a total area of approximately 13,000 (8080 miles) square kilometers. Most of the islands are surrounded by crystal clear, turquoise waters of the Atlantic Ocean, and are protected by coral reefs.

The Bahamas is an independent island nation and is part of the Commonwealth of Nations. Its capital, Nassau, is located on the island of New Providence, the most populated in the archipelago. The geographical location of the Bahamas is strategic, as it is at the center of the Caribbean cruise route and is a popular tourist destination.

# Short History

The Bahamas have a rich history dating back millions of years when the area was a coral reef that rose from the ocean. During the last ice age, the islands joined to form a single landmass known as the Bahamas Plain, which was covered by the sea after the ice melted. The area was uninhabited for thousands of years, until the arrival of the first settlers.

The first inhabitants of the Bahamas are believed to have been the Lucayans, a group of Arawak Indians who arrived on the islands around 1,000 years ago. The Lucayans lived by fishing, hunting, and gathering fruits, maintaining a peaceful and organized society. In 1492, the explorer Christopher Columbus landed in the Bahamas on his first voyage to the Americas, establishing the first European contact with the natives.

From that moment on, the Bahamas were colonized by the Spanish, the English, and the French, who disputed control of the archipelago for several centuries. In 1718, the British established the colonial government of the Bahamas, and the islands became a major center of trade and piracy in the Caribbean. During the American Revolution, the Bahamas were a refuge for those loyal to the British Crown and became a strategic point for trade with the British colonies in North America (Britannica, 2022; The Official Site of The Bahamas, 2021).

In the 20th century, the Bahamas became a popular tourist destination and in 1973, they gained their independence from the United Kingdom to become a sovereign nation within the Commonwealth. The Bahamas is currently a democratic state with a parliamentary system of government, headed by a Prime Minister and a Governor General representing the Queen of England as head of state (Bahamas Ministry of Foreign Affairs, 2021).

# Culture and Language

Bahamian culture is a mix of African, European, and American influences. Music, dance, and gastronomy are integral parts of Bahamian culture. Junkanoo is a form of music and dance that originated on the islands and is celebrated during the Christmas and New Year holidays. Bahamian food is based on fresh seafood and fish, such as conch (giant conch) and grouper (grouper), and is characterized by its hot and spicy flavor (Embassy of the Bahamas in Washington DC, 2021).

Bahamian society is multicultural and diverse, with a population of approximately 400,000. The majority of the population is of African descent, with a minority of European and Indian descent. The official language is English, although Creoles and regional dialects are also spoken. The predominant religion is Christianity, although there are also communities of practitioners of other religions (Embassy of the Bahamas in Washington DC, 2021).

The education system in the Bahamas is of quality and free for all citizens. Primary and secondary education is compulsory and higher education is available at various universities and colleges. The education system is managed by the Bahamas Ministry of Education and has a wide range of programs and activities to promote the academic and personal development of students (The Official Site of The Bahamas, 2021).

The government of the Bahamas is a constitutional monarchy and a parliamentary democracy. The Queen of England is the head of state, represented by the Governor General, and executive power is exercised by the Prime Minister, who is elected by Parliament. Legislative power is exercised by the bicameral parliament, which consists of the House of Representatives and the Senate.

The official language of the Bahamas is English, although creoles and regional dialects are also spoken. English is the language of instruction in schools and is widely used in business and government. In addition, Spanish is spoken by a significant part of the population due to its proximity to the Spanish-speaking countries of the Caribbean and Latin America (U.S. Department of State, 2022).

# Weather and Climate

The climate in the Bahamas is maritime subtropical, which means it has warm temperatures year-round, influenced by northeasterly trade winds and warm ocean currents. The average annual temperature ranges between 24 and 30°C, with a relative humidity of 80%. Throughout the year, two seasons can be distinguished: a wet season and a dry season.

The wet season in the Bahamas runs from May through October, with the highest temperatures recorded from July to August. During this time, the islands experience tropical storms and hurricanes. The humidity is high and the rains are frequent, especially in the afternoons and nights. However, the rains do not last all day and are not usually so strong as to significantly affect the planning of tourist activities.

The dry season in the Bahamas runs from November through April. During this period, the climate is drier and temperatures are cooler, averaging 21°C. The days are sunny and the nights are cool. It is the most popular tourist season and the best time to enjoy the beaches and outdoor activities.

It should be noted that, due to its geographical location, the Bahamas may be affected by global climate changes, which may lead to an increase in the frequency and severity of hurricanes and tropical storms (The Official Site of The Bahamas, 2021).

# Tourist Attractions in the Bahamas

In addition to the attractions already mentioned, there are many other things that visitors can enjoy during their stay.

In terms of museums, the National Museum of the Bahamas in Nassau is a must-see for those interested in the country's history. The museum has exhibits on the history of the Bahamas from prehistoric times to modern times, with an extensive collection of indigenous and colonial artifacts.

Bars and restaurants are also an important part of Bahamian culture. The Fish Fry on Arawak Cay in Nassau is a popular destination for local food, especially fresh fish and shellfish. In addition, the island of Eleuthera is known for its pineapple, and many bars and restaurants in the area serve drinks and cocktails made from this fruit (PlanetWare, 2023).

As for the beaches, in addition to those already mentioned, there are many other options to choose from. The Tropic of Cancer beach on the island of Exuma is one of the most impressive, with crystal clear waters and pink sand. Gold Rock Beach on Grand Bahama Island is also stunning, with a long stretch of white sand beach and crystal-clear waters.

Water activities are another top attraction in the Bahamas. Visitors can enjoy a wide variety of water sports, including snorkeling, scuba diving, paddle boarding, and fishing. Additionally, whale and dolphin watching is a popular activity at certain times of the year (Bucket List Journey, 2023).

For sports lovers, the Bahamas is also a popular destination for golf, tennis, and beach volleyball. Additionally, fishing is a popular activity in the Bahamas, with fishing tournaments taking place throughout the country throughout the year.

The national parks of the Bahamas are also major tourist attractions. The Exuma Cays National Park is one of the most popular, with an impressive variety of marine life and birds. In addition, the Lucayan National Park has a network of caves and underground caverns that visitors can explore.

Finally, exploring the flora and fauna is another popular activity in the Bahamas. Andros Island is known for its diversity of bird and butterfly species, while San Salvador Island is famous for its iguana population. Visitors can also explore the botanical gardens and nature reserves to learn more about the country's flora and fauna (Sandals, 2023).

## Accommodation

With a wide variety of accommodation options, there is something for every taste and budget. From luxury hotels to camping sites, here is an overview of the various accommodation possibilities in the Bahamas:

- **Luxury Hotels**: One of the most popular options in the Bahamas. There are many five-star hotels, such as the Grand Hyatt Baha Mar and the Atlantis Paradise Island Resort, that offer luxurious accommodations, a wide range of amenities, and exclusive services such as spas, gourmet restaurants, golf courses, and water parks.

- **All-Inclusive Resorts**: All-inclusive resorts are another popular option in the Bahamas. These resorts offer lodging, food, beverages, and activities in the same package, meaning guests don't have to worry about a thing during their stay. Some examples of all-inclusive resorts are the Sandals Royal Bahamian and the Meliá Nassau Beach.

- **Apartments and cabins**: If you are looking for something more private and cozy, you can choose to rent an apartment or a cabin. There are many options available in the Bahamas, and it is a good option for those who want more space and privacy. Some examples of sites to rent apartments or cabins include Airbnb, HomeAway, and VRBO.

- **Hostels**: If you are looking for a cheaper option, hostels are a good option. The hostels offer shared rooms and common bathrooms at very affordable prices. Some examples of hostels in the Bahamas include the Bahamas Backpackers Hostel and the Orange Hill Beach Inn.

- **Campgrounds**: For those looking for an outdoor experience, there are several camping options in the Bahamas. The campsites offer a unique nature experience, and there are options for all skill levels. Some examples of campgrounds in the Bahamas include the Andros Island Beach Resort and the Grand Bahama Island Campground (Taylor Boetticher, 2021; Marissa Sese, 2021).

# Souvenirs Worth Buying

When visiting this archipelago, there are many opportunities to purchase unique souvenirs and gifts that represent the culture and traditions of the Bahamas. Here is a list of the best gifts and souvenirs you can buy in the Bahamas:

- Straw crafts: They are one of the specialties of the Bahamas. The women of the islands have been weaving products from palm fronds for centuries. Straw craft options include straw hats, baskets, and bags.

- Bahamian Rum: A popular hallmark that you can purchase in the Bahamas. Well-known brands include Bacardi Rum, John Watling's Rum, and Bahamian Rum. Also, you can buy bottles with unique designs only found in the Bahamas.

- Bahamian Sands Rum Brand Products: Bahamian Sands Rum is a local alcoholic beverage that is also used to make several of the brand's products. These products include body creams, lotions, and bath products. They all contain rum as a key ingredient.

- Shell Crafts: Shells are one of the specialties of the Bahamas. Local artisans use shells to create a wide variety of products, including jewelry, fridge magnets, paintings, and ornaments.

- Local art: This is a good option if you want to go home with a memory of your paradise vacation, or take a souvenir to a loved one. Local artists create a variety of products, from paintings and sculptures to jewelry and decorative items.

- T-shirts and souvenirs: The typical and infallible popular souvenir option in the Bahamas. You can find t-shirts and souvenirs with the names of the islands and other representative designs of the Bahamas in gift shops and local markets.

- Coconut oil: This natural product is popular in the Bahamas, thanks to the abundant presence of this fruit. It is used in beauty and personal hygiene products and for cooking.

- Spices and Pepper Sauce: These culinary items are very popular in the Bahamas. You can find a variety of spice mixes as well as hot pepper sauces originating from the archipelago.

- Jewelry: Gold and silver jewelry are high-quality gift options in the Bahamas. Local designers create a variety of unique designs that represent the culture and history of the Bahamas.

- John Watling's Rum Brand Products: John Watling's brand of rum is iconic on the island, offering a wide variety of products from rum bottles to mugs and glasses (Carnival Cruise Line, 2021; Bahama Hand Prints, n.d.).

# Discovering Delicacies

The cuisine of the Bahamas is a combination of African, European, and American influences. Typical dishes are prepared with local ingredients and reflect the history and culture of the archipelago. Each bite is full of flavor, color, and tradition.

From the scent of spices in the air to the sound of hot oil in the pan, each Bahamian dish is a unique experience. The sweet and fresh flavor of the conch, a marine mollusk eaten raw in salads, is a delight for the palate. Fried fish is another typical dish, with a crispy batter and juicy, flavorful meat. Black pea soup is a comforting and flavorful dish, traditionally served at funerals and other ceremonies.

One of the most popular desserts in the Bahamas is rum cake, a moist and flavorful cake made with rum and spices. It's a sweet treat that reflects the rich history of the rum trade on the islands.

Bahamian food is not only delicious, but it is also an important part of the culture and society of the archipelago. Each dish reflects the national identity and cultural diversity of the Bahamas and is a way to connect with local people and traditions (Bahamas Ministry of Tourism, n.d.; Bahamas Food Tours, n.d.).

Food is like language: it offers the best of the diversity of each culture. If you visit the Bahamas, you cannot miss any of its typical fruits, dishes, and desserts. Here I list the most popular:

- Conch salad: This seafood salad is one of the most popular dishes in the Bahamas. The main ingredient is the snail shell chopped into small pieces and seasoned with lemon, orange, onion, pepper, and hot chili.

- Fish stew: A fish dish stewed in a tomato and spice sauce, served with rice and peas.

- Peas n' Rice: This dish is a kind of stew made with rice and peas, seasoned with garlic, onion, and pork or chicken.

- Macaroni and Cheese: A cooked pasta dish with a creamy sauce of cheddar cheese and spices.

- Johnny Cake: A sweet flatbread that is made with cornmeal, wheat flour, sugar, and butter.

- Potato Pie: A pie made of mashed potatoes mixed with cheese and onion, and baked in the oven.

- Black Pea Soup: A thick soup made with black peas, onion, carrot, and celery.

- Fried Fish: One of the most popular dishes in the Bahamas, consisting of fresh fish breaded and fried in hot oil.

- Goombay Smash: An alcoholic drink made with rum, pineapple, and orange juice.

- Rum Cake: A cake dessert drenched in rum and glazed with sugar (Princess Cruises, 2019, January 8).

These are just a few of the typical Bahamian dishes, but there are many more to try. If you are interested in learning more about the gastronomy of the Bahamas, you can visit websites such as the official page of the Ministry of Tourism of the Bahamas or the gastronomy section of the Bahamas Travel Guide magazine.

## Tips to Follow Before Visiting the Bahamas

If you are planning a trip to the Bahamas, there are several important things to keep in mind to ensure a smooth and pleasant travel experience. Here we provide you with information on visas, vaccinations, security, health, and budget so that you can prepare yourself properly before leaving:

- **Visas**: Citizens of most countries, including the United States, do not need a visa to enter the Bahamas as tourists. However, it is important to review the entry requirements according to the nationality of each traveler. For more information, you can visit the website of the Ministry of Foreign Affairs of the Bahamas (n.d.).

- **Vaccinations**: Specific vaccinations are not required to enter the Bahamas, but it is recommended to update routine vaccinations, such as measles, chickenpox, and hepatitis A and B. In addition, it is recommended to bring mosquito repellent and sun protection, since the hot and humid climate, in the Bahamas, is conducive to insect proliferation and sun exposure (Center for Disease Control and Prevention, 2022).

- **Safety**: The Bahamas is a safe tourist destination, but like anywhere in the world, visitors should be vigilant and take basic safety precautions. It is important to avoid carrying unnecessary valuables and keep personal belongings under surveillance at all times. It is also recommended not to walk alone at night and to avoid unfamiliar or dangerous areas.

- **Health**: Tap water in the Bahamas is safe to drink, but some visitors may experience an upset stomach due to the difference in the composition of the water and local foods. It is recommended to drink bottled water and follow healthy eating practices, such as washing hands before eating and choosing fresh, well-cooked foods (United States Department of State, 2022).

- **Budget**: The Bahamas can be an expensive destination, especially in touristy spots. Lodging, food, and activities can be more expensive than in other Caribbean destinations. However, there are inexpensive options available, such as Airbnb accommodation, transportation on local buses, and eating at street food stalls.

# Chapter 3: Martinique

Martinique Island is a true tropical paradise in the heart of the Caribbean. Its white sand beaches and crystalline waters, surrounded by a lush green landscape, are a gift for the senses. The island also has towering mountains, impressive waterfalls, and rich biodiversity that make it unique in the world. In the words of the Martinican poet Suzanne Dracius, "Martinique, the green jade in the necklace of the Antilles, this land of eternal spring, whose love song is a shower of flowers" (1998). Without a doubt, this island is an inspiring destination for any lover of nature and beauty.

## Location

The Martinique Islands are located in the Caribbean Sea, north of South America and southeast of Puerto Rico. The exact location of Martinique is between 14°26'N and 60°51'W (Google Maps, 2023).

The island of Martinique has an area of 1,128 km² (436 sq mi) and is located at a distance of 5,738 km (3,566 mi) from Madrid, Spain. The largest island of Martinique is located about 30 km (18 miles) north of Saint Lucia and about 40 km (25 miles) south of Dominica. The island of Martinique is surrounded by the Caribbean Sea to the west and the Atlantic Ocean to the east (WorldAtlas, 2023).

In addition to the main island, Martinique also has several small and uninhabited islands, such as the island of Saint Barthélemy, the island of Saint Lucia, and the island of Birds. The island of Saint Barthélemy is located northwest of Martinique and has an area of 25 km² (9.7 sq mi), while the island of Saint Lucia is located to the south of Martinique and has an area of 617 km² (238 sq mi). Bird Island is an uninhabited island located north of Martinique (Google Maps, 2023).

## Short History

Martinique Island is of volcanic origin and its formation occurred more than 25 million years ago. It is located in the contact zone between the South American plate and the Caribbean plate, which has given rise to a very rugged relief and the presence of numerous volcanoes.

The first inhabitants of Martinique Island were the Arawak and Carib Indians, who settled on the island about 2,000 years ago. These peoples were farmers and fishermen and lived in villages organized around a central *plaza* (square). Numerous archaeological traces of their presence have been found on the island, such as ceramics, utensils, and ritual objects.

Martinique Island was discovered by Christopher Columbus in 1502 during his fourth voyage, and was incorporated into the Spanish empire. However, the Spanish presence on the island was brief and in 1635 the island was colonized by the French, who turned it into a sugarcane plantation colony. For several centuries, the island was subjected to slavery and became one of the main centers of sugar production in the Caribbean.

Currently, Martinique Island is a French overseas territory, with a special status within the French Republic. It has its local government and its economy is based on tourism, agriculture, and fishing (Dubelaar, C. N., 2001).

## People and Culture

The people of Martinique are known as Martinicans, and although they are French citizens, they have a unique and vibrant culture that reflects the influence of their history and geography.

Martinicans are known for being friendly and hospitable, and their culture is characterized by a strong connection to nature and music. The island has beautiful beaches, rainforests, and mountains, and the people of Martinique have learned to live in harmony with their surroundings.

One of the most important festivities in Martinique is Carnival, which is celebrated in February or March, depending on the date of Easter. During Carnival, the island comes alive with music, dance, and costumes.

Martinicans dress up in colorful and elaborate costumes and join the processions that wind through the streets of the city. The Martinique Carnival is known for its drum troupes, which play traditional and energizing music.

Another of the most important cultural traditions in Martinique is food. The island is known for its Creole cuisine, which combines African, European, and indigenous influences. Typical dishes include Acra (fish fritters), boudin (blood pudding), Colombo (a spiced meat and vegetable stew), and Ti-Punch (a cocktail made with rum, lime, and sugar). Food is an important way of coming together and celebrating life for Martinicans.

Music is also an integral part of the Martinican culture, and the island has produced many famous artists in the zouk genre. Zouk is a musical genre that originated in the French West Indies in the 1980s, combining influences from reggae, salsa, and merengue. Martinicans are known for their love of music and dance, and it is common to see people dancing in the street during festivities and celebrations (Office de Tourisme de la Martinique, n.d.; Lonely Planet, n.d.).

## Species Found

This tropical paradise has a large number of endemic species of flora and fauna that are not found anywhere else in the world. Throughout history, explorers and scientists have been fascinated by the diversity of life on the island.

One of the most fascinating discoveries of the endemic flora of Martinique is the Tiare flower, also known as Gardenia taitensis. This flower is found only on the islands of the South Pacific and on the island of Martinique. It is said that it was discovered by the British navigator William Bligh in 1788 when he was on his way to the Pacific islands. Bligh brought some Tiare plants to Martinique, where they quickly adapted to the tropical climate and became one of the island's most iconic flowers.

As for fauna, Martinique is home to an endemic lizard species known as the Anolis Fuscoauratus. This lizard is known for its ability to change color depending on the environment it is in. The Anolis Fuscoauratus is believed to have originated in Martinique around 25 million years ago when the island broke away from the South American mainland.

Another fascinating endemic native to the island is the Martinique rattlesnake, also known as the Fer-de-Lance. This snake is unique in its appearance and venom and is believed to be one of the most dangerous animals on the island. Despite this, Martinicans have learned to live peacefully with the Fer-de-Lance, and many view the snake as a symbol of life on the island (Savage, J. M., 2002).

# Weather and Climate

Spring on Martinique Island is a warm and sunny time, with temperatures ranging between 24 °C and 28 °C. It is an ideal season to enjoy the beaches, practice water sports, and go on excursions around the island. Although it is a dry season, occasional showers are possible, especially in May. Don't worry, these are short, refreshing showers that usually last only a few minutes.

The Martinican summer is a hot and humid season, with temperatures that can reach 32 °C. It is an ideal time to enjoy the beaches and cool off in the sea, but also to explore the nature of the island since the frequent rain of the season keeps everything green and exuberant. The rains can be strong and prolonged, so it is recommended to wear waterproof clothing and shoes for excursions.

Autumn on the island is a transition season, with temperatures that drop slightly, ranging between 23 °C and 27 °C. It is a dry season, with little rain, which makes it an ideal time to explore the nature of the island and enjoy outdoor activities such as hiking and bird watching. It is also an ideal time to enjoy the gastronomy of the island since it is the harvest season for tropical fruits such as pineapple and mango.

The winter season—if it can be called winter—is a cool and dry season, with temperatures ranging between 21 °C and 25 °C. It is an ideal season to explore the island and enjoy cultural activities such as festivals and

Christmas events. Occasional showers are possible, especially in December, but overall it is a pleasant dry season (World Weather Online, 2021).

## Tourist Attractions in Martinique

Starting with the beaches, Martinique has some of the most beautiful in the Caribbean. The beaches of Les Salines, Anse Couleuvre, Grande Anse d'Arlet, and Anse Mitan are some of the most popular with tourists. On these beaches, you can enjoy activities such as diving, windsurfing, and paddleboarding, among other water sports.

In addition to the beaches, Martinique Island has a wide variety of recreational activities for the whole family. A place that you cannot miss is the Regional Natural Park of Martinique. This park has more than 6,000 hectares of land and is home to a wide variety of flora and fauna species. Here you can go hiking, bird watching, and enjoy the natural beauty of the island.

When it comes to history and culture, Martinique has a lot to offer. One place that you cannot miss is the city of Fort-de-France. Here you will find the Musée de la Pagerie, which is the house where Empress Josephine, wife of Napoleon Bonaparte, was born and raised. You can also visit Fort Saint-Louis, a fort built in the 17th century that has survived numerous battles and wars.

Another place that you cannot miss is the city of Saint-Pierre, which was destroyed by a volcanic eruption in 1902. Today, this city is an open-air museum where you can see the remains of buildings and monuments from that time.

When it comes to sports and recreational activities on the beach, Martinique has a wide variety of options. In addition to the water sports mentioned above, you can also play beach volleyball, soccer, and rugby (Comité Martiniquais du Tourisme, n.d.).

# Accommodation

When it comes to lodging options on Martinique Island, there is a wide variety of options ranging from luxury hotels to more affordable options. In this section, I briefly describe some of the options you might consider.

Starting with luxury hotels, Martinique has some of the best hotels in the region. The Hotel La Pagerie in Trois-Ilets is one of the most popular. This 4-star hotel offers a privileged location, with panoramic views of the Caribbean Sea and a wide variety of high-quality services. The French Coco Hotel in Tartane is another luxury hotel on the island, with beautiful rooms and villas surrounded by lush greenery.

As for cheaper accommodation options, there are plenty of hostels, guest houses, and apartments available. In the city of Fort-de-France, you'll find plenty of budget options, including the Hotel Bambou on Anse Mitan beach and the Bayfront Hotel in the city center.

There are also cheaper accommodation options in the beach areas, such as the Hotel Le Manguier in Les Trois-Ilets and the Hotel Corail Residence in Sainte-Luce. These hotels offer comfortable and affordable accommodation and are located close to some of the most popular beaches on the island (Comité Martiniquais du Tourisme, n.d.).

# Discovering Delicacies

Martinique's cuisine is characterized by a wide variety of ingredients and flavors that reflect the cultural diversity of the island. Below, I provide you with more details about some of the typical dishes and drinks on the island:

- Colombo: It is one of the most emblematic dishes of Martinique. It is a meat stew (chicken, fish, or pork) that is cooked with a mixture of spices called "Colombo." This spice blend is made up of cumin, coriander, turmeric, cloves, cinnamon, pepper, ginger, and garlic. It is also added to the preparation of vegetables, such as peppers, onions, tomatoes, and aubergines. The dish is usually accompanied by rice and sometimes with fried plantains.

- Boudin creole: It is a Creole sausage that is prepared with rice, pork, and various spices. It is served fried and can be found in markets and food stores throughout the island.

- Accras: They are small fried fish balls that are usually served as an appetizer in Martinique. They are made with fresh minced fish, onion, garlic, cilantro, and pepper, which are mixed with flour and fried in hot oil.

- Tourment d'amour: It is a very popular dessert in Martinique, consisting of a coconut cake with sugar and vanilla. The tart is baked in a puff pastry crust and can be found in many bakeries and pastry shops on the island.

- Tarte à la noix de coco: It is another coconut tart, but this one is prepared with a mixture of cream and grated coconut. The tart is baked in a pastry crust and can be found in pastry shops and cafes all over the island.

- Rum: The island of Martinique is known for its high-quality rum, which is produced from local sugar cane. There are several distilleries on the island, and rum is used as an ingredient in many cocktails and drinks, such as "Ti Punch".

- Ti Punch: It is a very popular alcoholic drink in Martinique. It is made with rum, fresh lemon juice, and sugar syrup. The cocktail is served in a small glass and sipped slowly to savor the flavors (Martinique, 2022).

# Chapter 4: Barbados

Barbados is a beautiful Caribbean island located to the east of the Lesser Antilles. The island is famous for its white sand beaches, crystal clear waters, and coral reefs. It is also known for its lush botanical gardens, rich colonial history, and lively culture. This jewel in the middle of the sea shines with its own light.

## Location

The island of Barbados is located in the Caribbean, specifically in the Lesser Antilles, east of the Leeward Islands. It is located at a latitude of 13.1939° N and a longitude of 59.5432° W. The island has an area of 430 km² (166 square miles) and a population of about 287,000.

To get to Barbados, you can take a flight to its international airport, Grantley Adams International Airport, which is located on the south coast of the island, about 16 km (10 miles) southeast of the capital, Bridgetown. The airport has connections with numerous cities in North America, Europe, and the Caribbean. It is also possible to reach Barbados by boat, as the island is a popular port of call for cruise ships (Britannica, 2022).

## Short History

The island of Barbados is a small island located in the eastern Caribbean, in the Lesser Antilles region. Its history dates back millions of years when the island was formed as an underwater volcano. As the volcano continued to erupt and grow, the island emerged from the water and became solid ground.

The first inhabitants of Barbados were the Amerindians, who arrived on the island around 1600 BC. These original peoples included the Arawaks and the Caribs, who settled on the island and called it "Ichirouganaim." They lived in Barbados for several centuries, hunting, fishing, and farming.

In the year 1625, the island was claimed by England, and a colony was established there. English colonists brought African slaves to work on the sugar and tobacco plantations they had established on the island. During the 17th and 18th centuries, Barbados' economy was heavily dependent on sugar production, and the island became one of the world's leading sugar producers (Britannica, 2021).

During the 19th century, Barbados went through a series of significant changes. In 1834, slavery was abolished throughout the British Caribbean, including Barbados. Many of the former slaves stayed on the island and worked as farm laborers on the plantations. In 1951, the first general elections were held in Barbados, and the country gained its independence from Great Britain in 1966. Since then, Barbados has been a stable democracy and has enjoyed sustained economic growth.

Today, Barbados is known for its white sand beaches, Caribbean music, and vibrant culture. It is also a major financial center and a popular tourist destination. Although the island has undergone many changes throughout its history, its natural beauty and rich culture continue to attract visitors from around the world (Visit Barbados, n.d.).

## People and Culture

The island has a rich history and culture that is reflected in its language, music, dance, religion, gastronomy, and popular traditions.

Barbados' culture is diverse and rich with African, British, and Caribbean influences. Music is an integral part of Barbadian culture, with calypso, soca, and reggae being some of the most popular genres. The official language is English, although Barbadian Creole, a variant of English with African and Caribbean influences, is also spoken.

The predominant religion in Barbados is Christianity, with the Anglican Church being the most important. However, there are also other religions such as Catholicism, Methodism, Adventism, and Pentecostalism. The Barbados carnival is one of the most important festivities on the island, celebrated in February or March, and includes parades, music, and dancing (Britannica, 2021).

Barbados' economy is based primarily on tourism and financial services. The island has a large number of hotels and resorts that attract millions of tourists every year. Furthermore, Barbados is a major financial center in the Caribbean, with a large number of banks and companies offering offshore banking services.

Other important economic activities are fishing, agriculture, and rum production. Fishing is a traditional activity on the island, with a large number of fishermen dedicated to catching different species of fish and shellfish. Agriculture is another important activity in Barbados, with the main crop being sugar cane, which is used to produce rum and other derived products.

The idiosyncrasy of Barbadians is characterized by their friendliness, hospitality, and respect for traditions. Family is a very important value in Barbadian society, and family ties are very strong. In addition, the island has a large number of popular festivities and traditions that reflect the rich culture of the island (Barbados, 2022).

# Weather and Climate

The climate of this island paradise is tropical, hot, and humid, with average annual temperatures ranging between 24 °C and 28 °C and relative humidity of 70%. The highest temperatures occur in July, August, and September, while the lowest is recorded in January and February.

The island of Barbados has two main seasons: the dry season and the wet season. The dry season begins in December and ends in May, while the wet season runs from June to November. During the dry season, the weather is generally dry and sunny, with occasional showers. Temperatures are often cooler than during the wet season, especially at night.

On the other hand, during the wet season, the island is more prone to tropical storms and hurricanes. Despite this, rainfall is usually short-lived and occurs mainly in the afternoon or night, which allows you to enjoy the beach for much of the day.

Barbados also has a windy season, known as the "easterly trade wind season." This season, which runs from November to June, is characterized by the presence of constant easterly winds that are usually mild and pleasant, making the temperature cooler and the climate more pleasant. During this season, there is also less chance of tropical storms or hurricanes (World Weather Online, 2021).

In general, Barbados has warm and sunny weather year-round, although visitors should be prepared for changes in weather conditions, especially during the wet season and in the event of tropical storms.

## Tourist Attractions in Barbados

The island of Barbados offers a wide variety of activities for all tastes and ages. From pristine beaches to historical museums, national parks, and activities related to the local flora and fauna, Barbados has something for all types of travelers.

One of the most popular activities on the island is visits to museums and historical sites. One of the most prominent museums is the Barbados Museum, located in Bridgetown. This museum has an impressive collection of objects related to the history and culture of the island, from pre-Columbian artifacts to objects from the colonial era. Another place of interest is the house of George Washington in Barbados, where the first president of the United States spent some of his youth.

Another popular activity in Barbados is exploring national parks. Farley Hill National Park is one of the most visited and boasts stunning panoramic views of the coastline and surrounding mountains. You can also take walks through the Graeme Hall Nature Reserve, which is home to a large number of species of birds and other animals.

The island also boasts a wide variety of beaches, from the popular white-sand beaches in the west to the quiet coves in the east. Prominent beaches include Crane Beach, Accra Beach, and Bathsheba Beach.

For those interested in the local flora and fauna, Barbados offers various nature-related activities. The Andromeda Botanical Garden is one of the highlights, with a wide variety of tropical plants and flowers, as well as an impressive waterfall. You can also take tours of the Welchman Hall Gully Nature Reserve, which is home to a wide variety of indigenous plants and animals.

Finally, for those interested in the geography of the island, you can take excursions along the coast to see the rock formations and sea caves, as well as inland to see the mountains and valleys (Visit Barbados, 2021).

# Accommodation

Barbados offers a wide variety of accommodation options to suit all tastes and budgets. Here is a selection of some of the most prominent options:

- **Luxury Hotels**: Barbados is known for its luxury hotels that offer first-class services and unforgettable experiences. One of the most prominent is Sandy Lane, a five-star hotel that has luxury suites and villas, a golf course, an infinity pool, a spa, and gourmet restaurants. Another luxury hotel on the island is the Fairmont Royal Pavilion, a beach resort that offers stunning ocean views, elegant rooms, and exclusive services.

- **All-Inclusive Resorts**: If you are looking for a worry-free vacation experience, all-inclusive resorts can be a great option. In Barbados, Sandals Barbados is one of the most popular resorts, offering a variety of activities such as water sports, cooking and yoga classes, and live entertainment. You can also opt for the Turtle Beach Resort, an all-inclusive hotel located on the south coast of the island that offers spacious suites and a wide variety of restaurants and bars.

- **Private Villas**: If you prefer to have your own space, renting a private villa may be the perfect option for you. The island has a wide variety of villas for rent, from small houses to luxury mansions. One of the most outstanding options is the Villa Bonita, a five-bedroom house with panoramic sea views, a private pool, and a privileged location on the west coast of the island.

- **Boutique Hotels**: For those looking for a more intimate and personalized environment, boutique hotels can be a great option. The Little Arches Boutique Hotel is one of the most popular on the island, with just 10 rooms and suites, a gourmet restaurant, and a prime location on the south coast of Barbados. Another notable boutique hotel is the Mango Bay Barbados, an all-inclusive beach hotel that offers comfortable rooms and a relaxed atmosphere.

- **Hostels**: For travelers with tighter budgets, the island has some cheap accommodation options, such as hostels and lodges. One of the most popular is the Casa Grande Airport Hotel, located near the airport and offering basic rooms at affordable prices. You can also opt for the Dover Beach Hotel, a budget hotel located on the south coast of the island that offers simple rooms and a privileged location near the beach.

In short, Barbados offers a wide variety of accommodation options to suit all tastes and budgets, from luxury hotels and all-inclusive resorts to private villas, boutique hotels, and budget options such as hostels and hostels.


# Delicacies to Explore


Barbadian food is a combination of African, indigenous, and European influences, resulting in unique and flavorful cuisine. Here are some of the most iconic dishes and drinks on the island:

- Local Fruits: Barbados is known for its wide variety of fresh fruits, including mangoes, avocados, bananas, pineapples, papayas, and guavas. It is also famous for its national fruit, the "barbados cherry" (acerola), which is rich in vitamin C and is used in drinks and desserts.
- Typical Dishes: One of the most emblematic dishes of Barbados is the "cou-cou and flying fish" which consists of a mixture of cornmeal and okra (a celery-like vegetable) served with fried fish. Other typical dishes include "macaroni pie" (macaroni pie), "rice and peas" (rice and beans), "pepperpot" (a meat and vegetable stew), and "pudding and souse" (a dish made with pork in a pickle and blood pudding).
- Sweets: The cuisine of Barbados has a wide variety of sweets and desserts, such as "sweet bread" (sweet bread made with fruits and spices), "coconut bread" (sweet bread made with coconut), and "rum cake" (cake made with rum and spices). Sweets made with cane molasses are also very popular, such as the "tamarind ball" (a ball made with tamarind pulp and molasses) and the "sugar cake" (a sweet made with grated coconut and molasses).
- Drinks: The most emblematic drink of Barbados is rum, which is produced locally and used in a wide variety of cocktails and drinks, such as "rum punch" and "mauby" (a drink made with tree bark and spices). Drinks made with fresh fruit are also popular, such as "guava juice" (guava juice) and "mauby juice" (mauby juice) (The Culture Trip, n.d.).

# Souvenirs Worth Buying

Barbados is an island rich in culture and traditions, making it a great place to find unique souvenirs, keepsakes, and gifts. Here are some of the most typical souvenirs and gifts from the island:

- Sugarcane Crafts: Sugarcane is one of the most important crops in Barbados, so crafts made from this material are very popular. Some examples of sugarcane crafts include baskets, hats, and decorative figures.

- Shell Jewelry: The island is also known for its beautiful beaches and rich marine life, which is why jewelry made from seashells is very popular. Necklaces, bracelets, and earrings are some of the types of jewelry that you can find.
- Rum Products: Barbados is the birthplace of rum, making it a great place to shop for rum-related products. Rum bottles, glasses, t-shirts, and other items with the logo of local rum brands are some of the options.
- Wood Crafts: Wood crafts are another popular form of souvenir in Barbados. From wood carvings to cutting boards to wooden bowls, there is a wide variety of wood crafts available on the island.
- Local Art: Barbados has a thriving arts community, making it a great place to find local art. Paintings, sculptures, and other forms of art are some of the options (Visit Barbados, n.d.).

## Tips to Follow Before Visiting Barbados

When traveling to Barbados, it is important to take into account several aspects related to visas, fees, health, and safety. Regarding visas, citizens of most countries do not need a visa to enter the island, although it is important to check the specific requirements for each country. In addition, a valid passport and a return ticket are required.

Regarding tariffs, Barbados applies a departure tax of 25 Barbados dollars (BBD) per person when leaving the country, which is normally included in the price of the plane ticket.

When it comes to health, Barbados has a modern and well-developed health system. However, it is recommended to have health insurance before traveling to be covered in case of any medical emergency. In addition, it is important to take preventative measures to avoid mosquito-borne diseases, such as Zika, Dengue, and Chikungunya. The use of mosquito repellent, protective clothing, and mosquito nets is recommended, especially in rural areas.

When it comes to security, Barbados is generally a safe place to travel, but it is recommended that you take some precautions to ensure the safety of yourself and your valuables. It is suggested not to leave valuables unattended on the beach or in public areas, avoid isolated and dark areas at night, do not accept drinks from strangers and always keep drinks in sight, and use official taxis and not take unidentified taxis.

Therefore, before traveling to Barbados, it is important to check visa requirements, be aware of fees, have health insurance, take preventative measures to avoid mosquito-borne diseases, and take some safety precautions to ensure a successful vacation. safe and enjoyable on this beautiful Caribbean island (U.S. Embassy & Consulates in Barbados, Eastern Caribbean, and the OECS, n.d.; Go Barbados, n.d.).

# Chapter 5: Saint Kitts

The Island of Saint Kitts is a tropical paradise that offers a unique combination of history, culture, and natural beauty. Its white sand beaches, crystal clear waters, and lush green landscapes are a dream come true for lovers of nature and adventure. In addition, its rich history and cultural heritage, including the fortified town of Brimstone Hill, are a source of inspiration for all those seeking an authentic and enriching experience. Discovering the Island of Saint Kitts is an experience that will transform the way you see the world and leave you with unforgettable memories that will last a lifetime (Discover St. Kitts, 2022).

## Location

Saint Kitts Island, also known as Saint Christopher, is an island located in the Eastern Caribbean. It is located northwest of the island of Antigua and southeast of Puerto Rico. It is part of the Leeward Islands and is part of the Lesser Antilles, an archipelago that stretches from southeastern Florida to Venezuela.

The island of Saint Kitts has an area of approximately 168 km² and is located approximately 2,160 km southeast of Miami, Florida. The island is shaped like a boomerang and features two volcanic peaks: Mount Liamuiga in the center and Mount Misery in the northwest.

The island of Saint Kitts is surrounded by the Atlantic Ocean to the east and the Caribbean Sea to the west. Its coasts are rugged in some areas and others have white sand beaches and crystal clear waters. In addition, the island has a wide variety of fauna and flora, including a large number of endemic species (Discover St. Kitts, 2022).

# Short History

The history of the Island of Saint Kitts dates back millions of years when it emerged from the ocean as a result of volcanic activity. For many centuries, the island was inhabited by indigenous tribes, including the Caribs and the Arawaks, who lived on the island until the arrival of the Europeans.

In 1493, Christopher Columbus sighted the island on his second voyage to the New World but did not land on it. It was the Spanish explorer, Juan Ponce de León, who in 1493 claimed the island for the Spanish crown. However, it was not until the 17th century that Europeans established permanent settlements on the island.

In 1623, the English established their first colony on the island and named it San Cristóbal, after the patron saint of sailors. Soon after, the French established themselves on the neighboring island of Nevis and began to dispute control of Saint Kitts with the English.

Over the next few centuries, the island of Saint Kitts witnessed numerous battles between the French and the English for control of the island and its thriving sugar industry. In 1783, the Treaty of Paris ended hostilities and gave the British sovereignty over the island.

Today, Saint Kitts is an independent state within the Commonwealth of Nations, although it remains a member nation of the Organization of Eastern Caribbean States (OECS). The island's economy is based on tourism, agriculture, and international trade.

In short, the history of the Island of Saint Kitts is rich and varied, from its geological emergence to the arrival of Europeans, conquest and clashes between colonizers, and independence to the present day as a sovereign state in the Caribbean (Discover St Kitts, 2022).

# People and Culture

The culture and idiosyncrasies of the Island of Saint Kitts are influenced by history and the mixture of African, European, and Caribbean cultures. The island's population is mostly descendants of enslaved Africans brought by Europeans to work in the sugar industry.

The official language of the island is English, although a local dialect known as "Kittitian Creole" is also spoken. This dialect is a mixture of English, French, and African, and is used in informal situations and local music.

Music is an important part of the culture of the Island of Saint Kitts, and the most popular music genre is calypso. The annual carnival is one of the largest celebrations on the island, featuring parades, music, dancing, and local food.

The island's gastronomy is a mix of African, European, and Caribbean influences. Local dishes include fresh fish, rice and beans, meat stews, and sweet plantains. Additionally, the island is known for its rum and tropical drinks.

Religion plays an important role in the life of the island's population, and the majority of the population is Christian. In addition, many religious festivities are celebrated throughout the year.

Regarding the idiosyncrasies of the population, the inhabitants of Saint Kitts are known for their friendliness and their sense of community. Family and religion are important values in the life of the people of the island, and hospitality is a prominent feature of the local culture.

As you can see, the culture of the Island of Saint Kitts is a mixture of African, European, and Caribbean influences, which is reflected in its music, gastronomy, religion, and traditions. The island's population is known for its friendliness and sense of community, and its local dialect, "Kittitian Creole," is a reflection of the island's cultural diversity (Discover St Kitts, 2022).

# Weather and Climate

In terms of climate, St. Kitts has a tropical savanna climate, with warm temperatures throughout the year and two main seasons: the wet season and the dry season.

The wet season on St. Kitts runs from May to November when most of the rainfall occurs on the island. During this time, humidity is high and temperatures range between 26 and 30 degrees Celsius. The rains can be quite heavy, averaging between 150 and 200mm of rain per month. Sometimes tropical storms or even hurricanes can occur.

On the other hand, the dry season in St. Kitts runs from December to April. During this time, the humidity drops, and temperatures can climb as high as 32 degrees Celsius. The rains are much less frequent, with an average of between 50 and 75 mm of rain per month.

Regarding the effects of global warming and the current climate crisis on the island of St. Kitts, some significant changes have been observed in its ecosystem. For example, an increase in water temperature has been observed around the island, which has affected marine biodiversity. The presence of fish species that were not previously found in the area has been recorded, as well as the decline of some coral species.

Additionally, rising sea levels have had an impact on the island's coastline. More rapid coastal erosion has been observed, leading to the loss of beaches and habitat degradation for some species.

Finally, the hurricane season in the Caribbean has become more intense in recent years, posing a threat to the island of St. Kitts. Hurricanes can cause significant damage to the island's infrastructure and economy, as well as endanger the safety of its inhabitants (World Weather Online, 2023).

## Tourist Attractions in Saint Kitts

Let's start with the bars and restaurants. One of the most popular places to enjoy good food and drink on St. Kitts is Fred's Bar and Grill in Frigate Bay. This place offers live music and delicious food and drink options. Fisherman's Wharf is another popular spot in Basseterre that offers great seafood and stunning views of the harbor. If you're looking for a more elegant setting, the Spice Mill Restaurant in Cockleshell Beach is a great option, with modern Caribbean cuisine and spectacular views of the Caribbean.

When it comes to museums and iconic places, the Brimstone Hill Fortress is one of the most visited places on the island. This UNESCO World Heritage Site sits on top of a hill and tells the story of the colonization of the island and its strategic importance during colonial times. Visitors can enjoy spectacular views of the Caribbean from the top of the fort.

Another iconic place on the island is the Church of the Immaculate Conception, located in Basseterre. This beautiful Catholic church was built in the 18th century and is one of the oldest structures in the city.

For those interested in nature, St. Kitts offers a variety of nature parks and reserves. South Friars Peninsula National Park is one of the most popular, with beautiful beaches, walking trails, and spectacular views of the Caribbean. The St. Kitts Botanical Garden is another popular venue, with a variety of tropical plants and flowers, as well as fish ponds and beautiful fountains (UNESCO, n.d.).

When it comes to cultural and recreational activities, St. Kitts offers a wide variety of options. Visitors can enjoy water sports such as scuba diving, snorkeling, and paddle boarding on the island's beautiful beaches. They can also enjoy nature walks, and guided tours of museums and historical monuments, as well as participate in cultural festivals such as the St. Kitts Music Festival or the annual Carnival (St. Kitts Tourism Authority, n.d.).

# Accommodation

The island of St. Kitts has a wide variety of accommodation options to suit all kinds of tastes and budgets.

As for luxury hotels, the Park Hyatt St. Kitts Christophe Harbor is one of the most prominent. This five-star hotel has spacious and elegant rooms, many of which have stunning views of the Caribbean Sea. In addition, it offers a wide range of luxury services and amenities, such as an infinity pool, a first-class spa, several restaurants and bars, a kids' club, and direct access to the beach.

Another luxury hotel on St. Kitts is the Four Seasons Resort Nevis. This five-star resort features a championship golf course, a luxury spa, several pools and restaurants, and direct access to a beautiful private beach. The rooms and suites are elegant and spacious, and many have spectacular views of the sea or the garden.

For those looking for a cheaper option, the island of St. Kitts has a variety of four-star hotels and hostels. The Marriott St. Kitts Beach Club is a popular option, offering spacious villas with full kitchens and access to a beautiful private beach. The Sugar Bay Club is another popular four-star hotel that has affordable rooms and suites, multiple pools, restaurants, and access to a nearby beach.

When it comes to apartments, St. Kitts has a plethora of options. The Royal St. Kitts Hotel offers spacious apartments with full kitchens, access to a nearby beach, and swimming pools. The Sealofts On The Beach is another popular apartment option that offers direct access to a private beach, pools, and beautifully landscaped gardens.

As for cheaper options, the island has several hostels and guest houses that offer affordable and comfortable accommodations. Culture House is a popular hostel offering simple rooms and a central location close to many restaurants and bars. The Ocean Terrace Inn is another popular option that offers affordable rooms and access to a pool and stunning views of the sea.

Finally, the island of St. Kitts also has a camping option at the Cades Bay campsite. This campground offers tents and access to a beautiful private beach.

When it comes to prices, luxury hotels in St. Kitts can cost between $500 and $1,000 per night, while four-star hotels and hostels can range from $200 to $400 per night. Apartments and guest houses are usually a bit cheaper, with prices ranging from $100-$200 per night. Campgrounds are the most affordable option, with prices ranging from $30 to $50 per night (St. Kitts Tourism Authority, n.d.).

# Discovering Delicacies

On the island, you can find dishes and drinks that fuse indigenous, African, European, and Asian influences.

As for fruits, one of the typical options is mango. This fruit is found in abundance on the island and can be enjoyed fresh, in juices, or as desserts. Other popular fruits on St. Kitts are papaya, pineapple, and coconut.

When it comes to drinks, rum is one of the most popular options. St. Kitts has its own distillery, Brinley Gold, which produces high-quality rums. Another popular cocktail is the "Painkiller" which contains rum, pineapple juice, orange juice, and coconut cream. In addition, the local beer, Carib, is also very popular on the island.

As for the typical dishes, one of the most popular is the "saltfish." This dish consists of salted cod that is cooked with local vegetables and spices. Goat water, a goat meat stew with vegetables and spices served with rice, is also common. Other popular dishes include the "conch fritter," deep-fried conch meatballs, and the "roti," a flatbread filled with chicken, meat, or vegetable curry (Caribbean Journal, 2018).

As for desserts, one of the most popular options is "guava cheese," This dessert consists of a mixture of guava and cheese that is cooked to a firm consistency. Another popular dessert is "bread pudding," a bread pudding made with old bread, milk, eggs, and spices.

Finally, in St. Kitts, you can also find local foods such as "christophene," a vegetable similar to zucchini, and "breadfruit," a fruit with a potato-like texture that is used in various dishes (St. Kitts Tourism Authority, n.d.).

# Souvenirs to Buy

The island of St. Kitts is a place full of cultural richness and natural beauty, which makes it a popular destination for tourists. In addition to its beaches and its gastronomy, the island has a wide variety of souvenir, gift, and souvenir options that reflect its culture and traditions.

One of the most popular options is local crafts. On the island, you can find hand-woven baskets, jewelry made with semi-precious stones, wooden sculptures, and ceramic items. These handicrafts are unique and reflect the island's rich history and traditions.

Another popular option is t-shirts and clothing items with the St. Kitts logo or images of the island. These items are a way to take home a tangible souvenir of the island and can be found in souvenir shops throughout the island.

In addition, local products are also a popular option to take as a souvenir or gifts. Rum from the local Brinley Gold distillery is a popular treat for spirits lovers, while ginger tea, a traditional island drink, is a popular choice for those looking for something different.

Finally, photos of the island and its panoramic views are one way to capture the natural beauty of St. Kitts. Local photographers sell their images in souvenir shops throughout the island and are a way to take home a lasting memory of the island (St. Kitts Tourism Authority, n.d.).

## Tips to Follow Before Visiting St. Kitts

Before traveling to the island of St. Kitts, it is important to consider several factors to ensure a safe and pleasant experience. Here are some things to consider before traveling to the island:

- Documentation and visas: Citizens of many countries, including the United States, the United Kingdom, and Canada, do not need a visa to enter St. Kitts if their stay is less than 90 days. However, a valid passport is required to enter the island. It is recommended to check the visa and documentation requirements before planning the trip.

- Travel insurance: It is advisable to purchase travel insurance before traveling to St. Kitts. This will cover any medical emergencies, lost luggage, or flight cancellations.

- Vaccinations: No specific vaccinations are required to enter St. Kitts. However, it is recommended to consult with a doctor about any necessary or recommended vaccinations before traveling.

- Climate: St. Kitts has a tropical climate, with hot and humid temperatures throughout the year. Hurricane season is from June to November, so it is recommended to monitor weather conditions before traveling.

- Currency: The official currency of St. Kitts is the Eastern Caribbean dollar (EC$). It is recommended to change some money before arriving on the island to pay for transport and other immediate expenses. You can also find ATMs on the island.

- Transportation: St. Kitts has an international airport, the Robert L. Bradshaw International Airport, and there are direct flights from several countries. The island can also be reached by ferry from other Caribbean islands. To get around the island, you can rent cars or use taxi services.

- Accommodation: There is a wide variety of accommodation options in St. Kitts, from luxury hotels to guest houses and apartments. It is recommended to book in advance to guarantee availability.

- Activities: St. Kitts offers a wide variety of activities for tourists, such as diving, snorkeling, catamaran rides, hiking, and visiting historical sites. It is recommended that you research and plan activities before you travel to make the most of your stay on the island (Lonely Planet, n.d.; Centers for Disease Control and Prevention, n.d.).

# Chapter 6: Negril

Negril Island, located on the west coast of Jamaica, is a true paradise on earth. With its white sand beaches and crystal clear waters, the island is a dream destination for lovers of the sun and nature. In addition to its impressive landscapes, the island offers a wide variety of activities, such as snorkeling, diving, boating, and hiking. With a relaxed and welcoming atmosphere, Negril is the perfect place to unwind and enjoy the natural beauty that the island has to offer. If you are looking for a destination to recharge your batteries and connect with nature, Negril is the ideal choice.

## Location

Negril Island is located on the west coast of Jamaica, in the Caribbean Sea. Geographically, it is located at the coordinates 18°15'N 78°20'W and has an area of 14.6 km². It is bordered to the north by Bloody Bay, to the east by the town of Green Island, to the south by the Caribbean Sea, and to the west by the city of Negril. The island is known for its stunning beaches, such as Seven Mile Beach, which stretches for 11 km and is considered one of the best beaches in the world. In addition, the island is surrounded by coral reefs that make it ideal for snorkeling and diving. Negril's location in the Caribbean makes it a popular tourist destination due to its warm climate and natural beauty.

## Short History

Negril Island is a small islet located in the Caribbean, off the coast of Jamaica. Its geological origin dates back to the Cenozoic era, approximately 65 million years ago, when the Caribbean tectonic plate began to move eastward and an uplift of the earth's crust occurred. This gave rise to the formation of the Blue Mountains, which span the entire island of Jamaica, and numerous islands and cays off its coast, including Negril Island.

The first inhabitants of Negril Island were animal species such as reptiles and prehistoric birds that inhabited the region in the Mesozoic era, more than 200 million years ago. Over time, the island was colonized by a wide variety of endemic species, including reptiles, birds, and mammals such as bats and monkeys.

The arrival of the first humans on the island of Negril occurred about 2,500 years ago, when the Arawaks, an Amerindian people who inhabited the Caribbean, arrived in the region. These people engaged in agriculture, fishing, and hunting, and built small settlements on the island's coast. During their stay on the island, the Arawaks developed a rich and complex culture and religion, which is reflected in the many caves and petroglyphs found on the island.

In the 15th century, the island of Negril was discovered by Spanish explorers, who named it "Isla de los Negros" because of the large number of African slaves that had been brought there to work on sugar plantations and other crops. Over the following centuries, the island was contested by various European powers, including the Spanish, English, and French, and was the scene of numerous battles and conflicts.

In the 18th century, the island of Negril became a British colony, and during the 19th and 20th centuries an economy based on the production of sugar, tropical fruits, and other crops developed. During this time, the island was also an important center of trade and piracy, and numerous ports and fortifications were built to protect against attacks by privateers and buccaneers.

Today, Negril Island is a popular tourist attraction, known for its beautiful white sand beaches, crystal clear waters, and water activities. The island has a wide variety of hotels, restaurants, and shops, as well as numerous tourist attractions such as the Negril Lighthouse, Green Island Cave, and Montego Bay National Park. Despite its tumultuous past, the island of Negril is today a peaceful and welcoming place, welcoming thousands of tourists each year in search of sun, sand, and relaxation (World Atlas, 2023; Britannica, n.d.).

# People and Culture

The island culture of Negril is influenced by Jamaican history and traditions but also has its unique idiosyncrasies and characteristics. The island's people are known for being friendly, welcoming, and laid-back, and pride themselves on their cultural heritage and easy-going, carefree lifestyle.

Music is an integral part of the island's culture, with reggae and dancehall being the most popular genres. Food is also an important part of the culture, and typical dishes include jerk chicken, fried fish, and rice with peas.

Politically, the island of Negril is part of the nation of Jamaica, which is a constitutional monarchy with a parliamentary system. Religion is also important on the island, with Christianity being the predominant faith, although there are also followers of other religions such as Rastafarianism.

The official language of the island of Negril and Jamaica, in general, is English, although patois, a variant of English that combines elements of African Creole and Spanish, is also spoken. The official currency is the Jamaican dollar, which is used both on the island and throughout the country.

In terms of the relationship of the people of the island of Negril with Jamaica, there is a strong sense of national identity and a strong feeling of solidarity with the rest of the country. However, the island also has its own unique identity and prides itself on its cultural heritage and unique way of life (Discover Jamaica, 2023).

# Weather and Climate

The island climate of Negril is typically tropical, with hot and humid temperatures throughout the year. However, there are some notable differences in the weather during the different seasons.

The rainy season on Negril Island begins in May and runs through November, peaking in September and October. During this time, the rains are frequent and often heavy, which can cause flooding and other problems in some areas. Temperatures during the rainy season are generally warm, averaging around 29°C.

The dry season on Negril Island begins in December and runs through April. During this time, the rains are much less frequent and temperatures are slightly cooler, averaging around 26-27 °C.

The island of Negril, like many parts of the world, is experiencing the impacts of climate change. Rising sea temperatures and changes in rainfall patterns are affecting the island's marine and terrestrial ecosystems. Sea level rise is also threatening coastal areas, including popular beaches like Seven Mile Beach.

Additionally, the island of Negril and Jamaica in general are prone to extreme weather events, such as hurricanes and tropical storms, which can cause significant damage to the island's infrastructure and ecosystems.

To address these issues, measures are being implemented to reduce greenhouse gas emissions and increase the resilience of ecosystems and communities to the impacts of climate change (Climate Analytics, n.d.).

## Places to Explore in Negril

One of the most popular natural attractions in Negril is Seven Mile Beach, which is a seven-mile stretch of white sand and crystal-clear waters, ideal for relaxing, sunbathing, and practicing water sports such as kayaking, paddle boarding, and water skiing. and snorkeling. In addition, you can also enjoy the sunset on the beach, which is a spectacular sight to see.

Another natural attraction is the Negril Hills National Park, where you can hike, bird watch, and enjoy the lush tropical vegetation. This park is also home to Green Island Cave, which is a limestone cave that can be explored on a guided tour.

For those interested in Jamaican history and culture, the Negril City Museum is a must-see. This museum houses artifacts, photographs, and documents that narrate the history of the city and the daily life of its inhabitants. There is also an exhibit on Jamaican Rasta culture and reggae music.

Another cultural attraction is the Rasta town of Bobo Hill, which is located in the foothills near Negril. This is a sacred place for Rastafarians, and visitors can learn about their religion, lifestyle, and music.

When it comes to recreational activities, there are plenty of options to choose from. Water sports are popular in Negril, as mentioned above, and you can also do activities like deep-sea fishing and parasailing. For those who prefer activities on dry land, there are options such as golf, tennis, cycling, and horse riding.

Nightlife in Negril is vibrant and exciting. There are several bars and clubs in the city, offering live music and dancing. One of the most popular places is Rick's Cafe, which is located on a cliff overlooking the sea. There, visitors can enjoy the sunset, live music, and cliff jumping (Visit Jamaica, (n.d.).

# Accommodation

There is a wide variety of accommodation options available to tourists, from luxury hotels to cheaper options such as apartments, cabins, hostels, and camping sites.

Starting with luxury hotels, one of the best and most exclusive is The Caves. This boutique hotel offers luxury bungalows built into cliffs overlooking the sea and features a swimming pool, spa, and award-winning restaurant. The Rockhouse Hotel is also a very popular luxury lodging option, with private cabanas, swimming pools, and a world-class restaurant.

For those looking for more affordable options, several hotels and hostels offer good value for money. The Xtabi Resort is a mid-range hotel that has affordable rooms and cabanas with sea views, as well as a pool and restaurant. The Negril Treehouse Resort is another affordable hotel with basic but comfortable rooms and cabins, as well as a pool and restaurant.

For those who prefer a more authentic experience, there are several apartments and cabins available for rent. Airbnb has a wide selection of affordable and authentic accommodation options, like Alice's log cabin in the woods or Shaun's apartment on the beach.

In addition, there are several campgrounds available in the Negril area, such as Barney's Flower & Hummingbird Garden, which has affordable campsites and rustic cabins surrounded by tropical gardens (Airbnb, 2023).

# Incredible Reasons You Must Visit Negril

There are many reasons why you should visit this beautiful island, from its breathtaking landscapes to its vibrant culture and rich history.

One of Negril's main attractions is its beaches, especially Seven Mile Beach. With its crystal clear waters and soft white sands, it is the perfect place for sunbathing, swimming, and water sports such as windsurfing and kayaking. Other popular beaches include Bloody Bay, Half Moon Beach, and Long Bay.

Another reason to visit Negril is its vibrant nightlife. The city has several nightclubs and bars, such as the famous Rick's Cafe, which offers live music and beautiful views at sunset. Additionally, Negril is known for its beach parties, where tourists can enjoy tropical drinks and Caribbean music under the stars.

In addition to its beaches and nightlife, Negril offers many other attractions for tourists. For example, the Kool Runnings Adventure Park is an amusement park that offers a variety of activities, including water slides, rafting, and an aquarium. You can also visit the Negril Lighthouse, which offers stunning panoramic views of the coastline.

Jamaican culture is also an attraction in itself. Tourists can visit the Bob Marley Museum in Kingston, which celebrates the life and work of the famous reggae musician. In addition, Negril offers many cultural festivals, such as the Reggae Sumfest and the Jamaica Food and Drink Festival (Visit Jamaica, 2023).

## Discovering Delicacies

Jamaican food is known for being savory and spicy, and Negril is no exception. Negril food is a combination of African, European, and native Jamaican influences, resulting in a variety of delicious and unique dishes.

One of Jamaica's best-known fruits is the ackee, which is the country's national fruit. This fruit is cooked with cod and served as a main course in many Negril restaurants. Another popular fruit in Negril food is the soursop, which is used to make drinks and desserts.

When it comes to drinks, Jamaica is known for its rum and Red Stripe beer. A popular drink in Negril is sorrel, a refreshing drink made with hibiscus flowers and spices like ginger and cinnamon. Another popular drink is rum punch, which is made from rum, lemon juice, and sugar.

One of the most popular dishes in Negril is jerk chicken. This dish is made with chicken marinated in a mix of Jamaican spices and grilled or grilled. Other popular dishes include goat curry, rice and peas, and fish escovitch, which is fried fish with onions, peppers, and vinegar.

As for desserts, tourists can try banana pudding, which is made with ripe bananas and spices like cinnamon and nutmeg. Another popular dessert is Jamaican carrot cake, which is made with grated carrots and spices like cinnamon and ginger (Lonely Planet, 2023).

## Shopping in Negril

Of course, if you go on vacation to a Caribbean island paradise, you will want to return home with a memory and bring gifts to your loved ones to share a part of your wonderful experience with them. Here I tell you all about the best souvenirs on the island and where to buy them:

Handmade jewelry is one of the most popular crafts on the Island of Negril. You can find beautiful pieces made of seashells, semi-precious stones, and hand-carved wood. Some of the most popular places to buy jewelry on the Island of Negril include:

- The Bob Marley jewelry store on Norman Manley Street.

- Janie's jewelry store downtown.

- Artisan Village is an arts and crafts market featuring a wide selection of handmade jewelry.

If you love handmade clothing and textiles, the Island of Negril is the place for you. Here you can find clothing items such as dresses, shirts, and skirts made from vibrant and colorful fabrics. In addition, you can also find beautiful woven rugs and handmade wall hangings. Some of the places to shop for clothing and textiles on the island are:

- The Wassy Wear clothing store on Norman Manley Street.

- The Negril T-Shirt Company textile store on West End Street.

- Jamaica Tammy's beachwear store on Norman Manley Street.

Hand-carved wood is another of the most popular crafts on the Island of Negril. Here you can find animal sculptures, jewelry boxes, and other objects hand-carved by local artisans. Some of the places to buy wood crafts are:

- The Caribic House wood crafts shop on Norman Manley Street.

- The Caribbean Craft Market wood crafts store on West End Street.

- The Rasta Muffin wooden crafts shop on West End Street.

The Island Negril is renowned for its vibrant street art scene. Here you can find colorful and expressive murals and graffiti that tell stories about culture and life in Jamaica. Some of the places to see street art are:

- The graffiti wall on Norman Manley Street.

- Murals on the beach at Seven Mile Beach.

- The painted walls at the Artisan Village craft market (Moore, C., 2020).

# Tips to Follow Before Visiting Negril

Before visiting Negril, there are several important things to keep in mind so that you can enjoy your trip to the fullest. Here are some of the most important things you need to know:

Regarding visas and entry requirements to the country, you should know that citizens of most countries do not need a visa to enter Jamaica. However, you must check the specific entry requirements for your country at the Jamaican Embassy in your home country.

The official currency of Jamaica is the Jamaican dollar (JMD). It is advisable to change some money at the airport upon arrival, although there are also ATMs and exchange houses in Negril. However, many places accept US dollars, so you may not need to exchange much local money.

There are several transportation options on the island. You can take a taxi from the airport or rent a car. You can also opt for local transport services, such as minibusses and shared taxis. However, be aware that the roads in Jamaica can be dangerous and drivers often drive aggressively.

The best time to visit Negril is between December and April, as it is the dry season and there is less chance of rain. However, this also means that it is the high season, so prices may be higher. If you prefer to avoid crowds, it is best to visit the island during the low season, which runs from May to November.

Before traveling to Negril—or any other destination—it is recommended that you contact your doctor to ensure that you are up to date on all recommended vaccinations. Also, keep in mind that malaria and dengue fever are mosquito-borne diseases in Jamaica, so you must take steps to protect yourself from mosquito bites, such as using insect repellent.

To rent a car in Jamaica, you will need a valid driver's license and a passport. It is also important to note that driving is on the left side of the road in Jamaica (Embassy of Jamaica, n.d.).

# Chapter 7: Puerto Rico

Puerto Rico is an island of exuberant natural beauty, located in the Caribbean. With its white sand beaches and crystal clear waters, the island offers a wide variety of water activities, such as diving and surfing. The vegetation is impressive, with tropical forests full of life and majestic mountains, such as El Yunque, the only tropical forest in the territory of the United States. It is also home to a wide variety of fauna, including iguanas, coquíes, and exotic birds. The natural wealth of Puerto Rico is a treasure that must be protected and valued for future generations.

## Location and How to Get There

Puerto Rico is located in the Caribbean Sea, east of the Dominican Republic and west of the Virgin Islands. It is an unincorporated territory of the United States and is located approximately 1,000 miles southeast of Miami, Florida.

There are several options to get to Puerto Rico. The most common way is by plane, since the Luis Muñoz Marín International Airport in San Juan, the island's capital, is an important transportation hub with connections to many destinations around the world. There are also airports in other parts of the island, such as Aguadilla and Ponce, that offer international and domestic flights.

Another option to get to Puerto Rico is by boat. There are several major ports on the island, including the port of San Juan, which is one of the largest cruise ports in the Caribbean. Visitors can also arrive via ferry from the Virgin Islands or the Dominican Republic (Discover Puerto Rico, 2021).

## Short History

The island of Puerto Rico has a rich and complex history that goes back millions of years. Geologically speaking, Puerto Rico was formed about 145 million years ago through tectonic and volcanic activity in the Caribbean region. During this time, various mountains and valleys were formed on the island, and soil erosion and sedimentation created a great diversity of ecosystems.

Before the arrival of humans, Puerto Rico was inhabited by a variety of animal and plant species. Fossils found on the island indicate that there were giant mammals such as the Megalocnus, a type of ground sloth, as well as animals such as the Jaguar and the Caiman. In addition, the island was home to a large number of endemic birds and reptiles, such as the Coquí, a small frog that is a cultural symbol of the island.

The first human inhabitants of Puerto Rico arrived approximately 4,000 years ago. These first settlers are believed to have been Arawak and Taino Indians, who arrived via the Greater Antilles from South America. The Taínos, in particular, were expert farmers and fishermen, and they created a vibrant and complex culture on the island. The island was known as Borinquen, which means "the land of the brave and noble lords."

The arrival of the Europeans in 1493, led by Christopher Columbus, changed the history of Puerto Rico forever. The Spanish began to colonize the island and exploit its resources, including the indigenous labor force. Unfortunately, the Taínos suffered a tragic population decline due to disease and mistreatment by colonizers, leading to their eventual extinction.

In 1898  Spain ceded Puerto Rico to the United States, after the Spanish-American War, Thereafter, the island has been an unincorporated territory of the United States and has been under its political rule. During the 20th century, Puerto Rico experienced rapid economic development, driven in large part by the pharmaceutical industry and chemical manufacturing. However, the island has also experienced social and political problems, including the fight for equal rights and independence.

Today, Puerto Rico remains an unincorporated territory of the United States, and its political status remains a controversial issue. The island has a diverse economy, including tourism, manufacturing, and services, but also faces economic and social challenges. In addition, the island has been affected by natural disasters, including hurricanes and earthquakes, which have aggravated its economic and social problems (Britannica, 2021; Puerto Rico Herald, 2003).

# Weather and Climate

Puerto Rico has a tropical climate that is characterized by being hot and humid throughout the year, with temperatures ranging between 21 and 33 °C. The island is located in an area prone to hurricane formation, which means that the weather can be quite unpredictable and variable, especially during the hurricane season, which runs from June to November.

During the summer months, the island experiences higher temperatures and an increase in humidity. The easterly trade winds are constant throughout the year, and during the summer months, they can be stronger, helping to mitigate the high temperatures. Rainfall is also more frequent during the summer months, with rainfall that can be quite heavy. Hurricane season begins in June and ends in November, with a higher chance of storms and hurricanes between August and October (Britannica, 2021).

During the winter months, the island experiences cooler temperatures and a decrease in humidity. The trade winds are less strong, allowing high-pressure systems from the North Atlantic to move south and affect the island's weather. This can bring with it dry and hot weather conditions.

Puerto Rico's climate has a significant impact on the island's economic activities. Agriculture, for example, is highly dependent on weather and rainfall. During the summer months, farming becomes more difficult due to heavy rains and humidity, which can make harvesting crops more difficult and increase the likelihood of plant diseases. On the other hand, the winter season can be more favorable for agriculture due to the dry and cooler weather.

Tourism is also affected by Puerto Rico's weather. During the summer months, beach tourism is very popular, but hurricane season can affect reservations and travel plans. Furthermore, tourists can also avoid visiting the island during the summer months due to the hot and humid climate.

Regarding the impact of climate change on the island, Puerto Rico is expected to experience an increase in the frequency and intensity of extreme weather events, such as storms and hurricanes. This can have a negative impact on the flora and fauna of the island, as well as on the economy and human activities in general (García-Quijano, J. F., Comarazamy, D. E., & Ochoa-Martínez, C. I., 2019).

# Tourist Attractions in Puerto Rico

Puerto Rico is a very popular tourist destination in the Caribbean, with a rich history and culture, impressive natural sites, and lively nightlife. There is plenty to see and do on the island, from exploring its national parks to visiting its historic sites to enjoying its beaches and outdoor activities. Below are some of the main places and tourist activities in Puerto Rico.

Puerto Rico has an impressive variety of natural places and national parks to explore. One of the most popular is El Yunque, the only tropical rainforest in the US national park system. Visitors can explore its many waterfalls, trails, and natural pools, and observe a wide variety of flora and fauna.

Another popular natural spot is Bioluminescent Bay, on the island of Vieques, where visitors can experience the magical phosphorescent light produced by microorganisms in the water. The Cabezas de San Juan Nature Reserve in Fajardo is another place to observe the flora and fauna of Puerto Rico, including the spectacular bioluminescent lagoon of Las Croabas.

Puerto Rico has a rich history and culture, and there are many historical places to visit throughout the island. In the capital, San Juan, visitors can walk the narrow streets of the old city and visit Fort San Felipe del Morro and Fort San Cristóbal, two impressive 16th-century Spanish fortifications. Also in San Juan, is the Castillo de San Juan de la Cruz, a 17th-century fortification on the island of Vieques.

In Ponce, visitors can visit the Museo de Arte de Ponce, which has an impressive collection of European and Latin American art, as well as the Casa Armstrong-Poventud, a well-preserved example of Puerto Rican neoclassical architecture. In Arecibo, there is the Cathedral of San Felipe Apóstol, the oldest church in Puerto Rico, built-in 1616.

Puerto Rico is also known for its lively nightlife, especially in the capital, San Juan. Visitors can enjoy live music at many clubs and bars in Old San Juan and in the Condado area. The Plaza del Mercado in Santurce is also a popular place to enjoy local food and live music.

On the west coast of the island, in Rincón, visitors can enjoy surfing on some of the best beaches in the Caribbean, such as Playa Domes and Playa Tres Palmas. There are also many options for snorkeling and diving on the island, including the Culebra Island Marine Protected Area.

In summary, Puerto Rico is a complete tourist destination, with a wide variety of places and activities to enjoy, from exploring its national parks and historical places to its lively nightlife and impressive beaches. Puerto Rico is a very popular tourist destination in the Caribbean, with a rich history and culture, impressive natural places, and lively nightlife. There is plenty to see and do on the island, from exploring its national parks to visiting its historic sites to enjoying its beaches and outdoor activities. Below are some of the main places and tourist activities in Puerto Rico.

As you can see, Puerto Rico is a complete tourist destination, with a wide variety of places and activities to enjoy, from exploring its national parks and historical places to its lively nightlife and impressive beaches and outdoor activities. The island is also famous for its gastronomy, with a unique mix of Spanish, African, and Taino influences. Visitors can enjoy typical dishes such as rice with gandules, mofongo, and roast suckling pig, as well as local drinks such as rum and piña colada (Puerto Rico Tourism Company, 2023).

It is important to note that, in addition to its tourist attractions, Puerto Rico also has a complex and unique political and economic history as an unincorporated territory of the United States. The island has gone through several important moments in its history, including the arrival of the Spanish conquistadors in 1493, the abolition of slavery in 1873, and US statehood.

## Visiting Cueva Del Indio

La Cueva del Indio is a tourist attraction located in the municipality of Arecibo, on the north coast of Puerto Rico. It is known for its stunning views of the Atlantic Ocean and its fascinating geological and archeological history.

The cave is part of the Arecibo National Park cave system and is considered one of the most spectacular. The cave is made up of limestone and is approximately 200 feet in length. The cave entrance is an opening in the cliff facing the ocean.

The history of the cave dates back thousands of years when the Taíno Indians inhabited the island. The Taínos were indigenous people who inhabited the Greater and Lesser Antilles before the arrival of the Spanish in 1493. The cave was used by the Taínos as a sacred place where they performed ceremonies and rituals.

During the Spanish colonial era, the cave was used as a refuge by Taíno rebels who fought against the conquistadors. In the 1700s, the cave was used by smugglers as a hideout for their wares.

In the 1930s, the cave was used as an entertainment venue by the Garcia family, who built a small platform inside the cave to enjoy views of the ocean. In the 1960s, the cave was opened to the public as a tourist attraction.

The cave has been the subject of several anthropological and archaeological studies. In the 1960s, archaeologist Ricardo E. Alegría excavated the cave and discovered various Taíno objects, including necklaces, stone axes, and ceramic plates. Human remains were also found, suggesting that the cave was used as a burial site (Discover Puerto Rico, n.d.).

In the 1980s a geological study was carried out which revealed that the cave had been formed millions of years ago by ocean erosion. It was also discovered that the cave is located on top of an underground aquifer, making it an important source of freshwater for the region (Vega-Pérez, J., 2014).

Today, the Cueva del Indio is a popular tourist attraction in Puerto Rico. Visitors can walk inside the cave and enjoy the amazing views of the ocean. It is also possible to do outdoor activities, such as hiking, kayaking, and surfing on the nearby beaches (González-Rivera, M., 2012).

# Accommodation

Puerto Rico is a popular tourist destination that offers a wide range of accommodations, from luxury hotels to hostels and campsites. In this detailed description, I will introduce you to some of the best accommodations in Puerto Rico.

Luxury hotels in Puerto Rico are a popular choice for those looking for a high-end vacation experience. One of the most popular is the Ritz-Carlton, San Juan, located on the beach in Isla Verde. The hotel features an outdoor pool, a luxury spa, and several dining options, including an Italian restaurant and a local cuisine restaurant. Another popular option is the St. Regis Bahía Beach Resort, which boasts a beachfront location on the east coast of Puerto Rico. The hotel features an outdoor pool, a luxury spa, and an 18-hole golf course designed by Robert Trent Jones Jr.

For those looking for a more modest housing experience, apartments in Puerto Rico are a popular option. One of the most popular is the Ocean Park Studios, located in the Ocean Park neighborhood of San Juan. Apartments feature full kitchens, air conditioning, and access to a rooftop terrace with ocean views. Another popular San Juan apartment is the San Juan Beach Apartments, which boasts an oceanfront location on Condado Beach and offers access to an outdoor pool and sun terrace.

For those looking for a cheaper lodging experience, hostels in Puerto Rico are a popular option. One of the most popular is the Mango Mansion, located in the Ocean Park neighborhood of San Juan. The hostel has shared private rooms, a shared kitchen, and access to a rooftop terrace with ocean views. Another popular hostel in San Juan is the Posada San Francisco, which is centrally located in Old San Juan and offers private and shared rooms.

Finally, for those looking for a more natural and affordable lodging experience, camping in Puerto Rico is a popular option. One of the most popular campgrounds is the El Yunque National Forest Campground, located in the rainforest of the El Yunque National Forest. The campground has tent sites and a picnic area. Another popular campground in Puerto Rico is Campamento Piñones, located on Piñones beach in Loíza and offers beach access and a picnic area (Airbnb, 2023).

# Discovering Delicacies of Puerto Rico

Puerto Rican gastronomy is a fusion of indigenous, African, and Spanish influences, which has evolved throughout the island's history. The basic ingredients of Puerto Rican cuisine include plantains, yucca, rice, beans, pork, shellfish, and spices such as achiote and cilantro. In this narration, I will talk about the typical dishes, desserts, and drinks of Puerto Rico, as well as the importance of gastronomy in the country.

Typical dishes:

- Arroz con gandules: This is one of the most emblematic dishes of Puerto Rico and is served as a side to many other dishes. It is a rice dish with pigeon peas (peas), pork, and a variety of spices such as coriander, achiote, and cumin.

- Mofongo: it is a ball of mashed green plantain mixed with garlic and pork rinds. It can be filled with meat, seafood, or vegetables. It is one of the most popular dishes on the island.

- Roast suckling pig: this is a whole pig roasted for several hours and served with rice and beans.

- Pastels: they are a kind of tamale made with plantain dough stuffed with meat, pork, or vegetables.

- Asopao: It is a rice stew similar to a soup and can be made with chicken, seafood, or meat.

Typical desserts:

- Flan: it is a dessert made with eggs, condensed milk, and caramel. It is one of the most popular desserts in Puerto Rico.

- Tembleque: it is a dessert made with coconut milk, cornstarch, and sugar. It has a consistency similar to flan but is thicker.

- Arroz con dulce: it is a dessert made with rice, coconut milk, cinnamon, ginger, and raisins.

- Quesito: it is a sweet cheesecake that is served with a puff pastry.

- Mantecaditos: these are vanilla-flavored shortbread cookies sprinkled with powdered sugar.

Typical drinks:

- Coquito: it is a drink made with coconut milk, rum, condensed milk, cinnamon, and nutmeg. It is very popular during the Christmas holidays.

- Piña colada: it is a drink made with pineapple, rum, and coconut milk. It is a very refreshing drink on the island.

- Medalla: it is a local beer that is very popular in Puerto Rico.

- Sangria: it is a drink made with red wine, fruits, and juices.

The importance of gastronomy in Puerto Rico is enormous. Puerto Rican cuisine is a form of cultural expression and a unifying element that connects Puerto Ricans of all social classes and regions. In addition, gastronomy is an important industry in the country's economy and is a major tourist attraction. Puerto Rico has a large number of restaurants and gastronomic festivals, such as the Saborea Puerto Rico Gastronomic Festival and the Mojo Isleño Festival in Salinas, which attract tourists from all over the world (Rodriguez, M., 2019; Saborea Puerto Rico, n.d.).

# Tips to Follow Before Visiting Puerto Rico

Next, I will provide you with all the information you need to know before traveling to Puerto Rico.

If you are a citizen of the United States, you do not need a visa to travel to Puerto Rico, since it is an unincorporated territory of the United States. If you are a citizen of another country, you should verify if you need a visa to enter the United States and meet the requirements (US Department of State, n.d.).

The official currency of Puerto Rico is the US dollar (USD). It is important to carry enough cash or use credit/debit cards, as some establishments do not accept card payments.

The official language of Puerto Rico is Spanish, although English is widely spoken on the island, especially in tourist and commercial areas.

Puerto Rico is generally safe for tourists, but like anywhere, it's important to take basic safety precautions. Some recommendations include:

- Do not walk alone in unfamiliar or poorly lit areas, especially at night.

- Do not leave valuables unattended on beaches or public places.

- Do not carry large amounts of cash or valuable jewelry.

- Pay attention to the warnings of the local authorities in case of extreme weather conditions.

No special vaccinations are required to travel to Puerto Rico, but it is advisable to be up to date with routine vaccinations. Tap water is safe to drink in most areas of Puerto Rico, but it's best to check with local authorities if there are any restrictions in the area where you'll be staying. It is also recommended to bring insect repellent to prevent mosquito bites and other pests (Government of Puerto Rico, n.d.).

# Chapter 8: Dominica

Dominica is an island in the Caribbean that is known for its stunning natural beauty. The island is home to lush tropical forests, breathtaking waterfalls, vibrant coral reefs, and black sand beaches. The crystal clear rivers of the island are another of its natural charms, and some of them include natural pools where visitors can swim. In addition, Dominica is a paradise for wildlife lovers, with a wide variety of unique animal and plant species. Dominica's beauty is truly breathtaking, and it is an ideal destination for those seeking an escape to a natural paradise in the Caribbean.

## Location

Dominica is a small Caribbean island located in the Lesser Antilles, specifically in the Windward Islands group. The island covers an area of 290 square miles (751 km²) and is located at latitude 15°25′N and longitude 61°20′W.

The island of Dominica is located in the Caribbean Sea, between the islands of Guadeloupe to the north and Martinique to the south. To the west is the Caribbean Sea and to the east is the Atlantic Ocean. Its coastline is 148 miles (238 km) in length and has a large number of bays, inlets, and beaches.

Regarding territorial waters, Dominica has 200 nautical miles (370 km) wide Exclusive Economic Zone (EEZ), giving it exclusive rights to natural resources, including fisheries and energy resources, within that area. In addition, the island also has a continental shelf that extends beyond its territorial waters.

Dominica does not share land borders with any country but is close to several neighboring countries in the Lesser Antilles, including Guadeloupe and Martinique to the north, Saint Lucia to the south, and Saint Vincent and the Grenadines to the south (Britannica, 2023; Google Maps, 2023)

# Short History

The history of this island is long and fascinating, dating back millions of years when it was formed as a result of volcanic activity. In this section, the history of Dominica will be explored in depth, from its geological formation to its political, economic, and social modernity.

The island of Dominica is of volcanic origin and its formation began about 25 million years ago, during the Eocene era. The island lies in a subduction zone, where the Caribbean tectonic plate dips below the Atlantic plate. Volcanic activity on the island has been constant for millions of years and has resulted in rugged and mountainous topography.

According to geological studies, the island of Dominica is composed of several layers of volcanic materials. The upper layer is made up of ash and pumice, while the lower layer is made up of igneous rocks. The oldest volcanoes on the island are in the northern region and are the most eroded. The youngest and most active volcano is the Morne Diablotins volcano, located in the center of the island.

The island of Dominica has been home to various species of animals and plants throughout its geological history. Fossil records have shown that animals such as mammals, birds, and reptiles once existed on the island. Fossils of mammals such as the Capuchin monkey and the giant sloth, which lived on the island thousands of years ago, have been found (Paul Crask, 2014).

Reptile fossils have also been discovered, such as the Dominica iguana, an endemic species found only on the island. In addition, fossils of extinct birds have been found, such as the Amazon arausiaca, a species of parrot that inhabited the island many years ago.

Human presence on the island of Dominica dates back some 4,000 years when the first pre-Columbian settlers arrived on the island. These first inhabitants were Arawak Indians, who had arrived from South America. The Arawaks settled on the island and created a society based on agriculture and fishing.

For centuries, the Arawaks lived on the island, developing their own culture and adapting to the environment. However, in the 15th century, the Caribs, a warlike indigenous tribe, invaded the island and displaced the Arawaks. The Caribs were known for their skill in warfare and their prowess in navigation.

In the 17th century, Europeans began to explore and colonize the Caribbean. The island of Dominica was one of the territories colonized by the Europeans, being claimed first by the French and then by the British. During colonial times, the island was used primarily for the production of sugar and other cash crops. British colonists brought African slaves to work on the plantations, resulting in a divided and unequal society.

The fight for independence began in the 1930s when farm workers began to organize and fight for better working conditions and political rights. In 1967, Dominica became an associate state of the United Kingdom, and in 1978, it gained full independence. Since then, the island has undergone a process of political, economic, and social modernization.

Today, Dominica is a parliamentary republic with a diversified economy, including tourism, agriculture, and the financial sector. The island has managed to protect much of its environment, conserving a large number of forests and natural areas.

In addition, the island has managed to develop sustainable tourism, based on ecotourism and the preservation of nature. Dominica is known for its beautiful beaches, its rich biodiversity, and its vibrant culture.

The exploitation of the island by the British during the 18th and 19th centuries had a significant impact on the island's population and environment. However, the island's independence and modernization have allowed Dominica to become an example of how a country can protect its environment and develop a sustainable economy.

It is important to recognize Dominica's rich history and continue to work to protect its environment and foster its economic and social development in a sustainable and equitable manner (Lennox Honychurch, 1995).


# Culture and Language

Dominica's culture is largely based on the island's relationship with nature and the environment. Dominica's people have maintained a close relationship with their natural environment, which is reflected in the way they dress, their music, their art, and their food. The island also has a rich history, dating back to the indigenous peoples who inhabited it before the arrival of Europeans.

Dominica's traditions are largely centered around religion and celebrations. The predominant religion on the island is Christianity, particularly the Catholic Church. Religious celebrations, such as Easter and Christmas, are very important to the island's population and are celebrated with great enthusiasm and fervor.

Another important tradition in Dominica is that of the carnival festivities, which are celebrated in February before the start of Lent. Dominica's carnival is known for its colorful and vibrant music, dance, and parades.

The official language of Dominica is English. However, the island's population also speaks Creole, a creole language based on English and with African and French influences. Creole is widely used in daily life on the island and is an important part of Dominica's culture.

Music is an integral part of Dominica's culture. The island has a long musical tradition dating back to the indigenous peoples who inhabited it before the arrival of Europeans. The traditional music of Dominica is heavily percussion-based, with drums and other percussion instruments used to create rhythms and melodies.

One of Dominica's most popular musical genres is cadence-lypso, a fusion of traditional Caribbean and African music with Western popular music. The cadence-lypso is vibrant and energetic music that is played all over the country.

Dominica's traditional dances rely heavily on percussion and music. The most popular dances include the bélé, the quadrille, and the heel-and-toe. The bélé is a folk dance of African origin that is performed with drums and maracas. The quadrille is a dance of European origin that is performed in pairs and is accompanied by live music. Heel-and-toe is an energetic dance performed in a group to the accompaniment of drums and other percussion instruments (Discover Dominica, n.d.; Britannica, 2023).

# Weather and Climate

Its climate is characterized by being tropical, with high temperatures and high humidity throughout the year. The island has two seasons: the dry season and the wet season. The dry season runs from December to May, and the wet season runs from June to November.

During the dry season, the weather is generally hotter and drier, with temperatures ranging between 26 and 30 degrees Celsius. Humidity is relatively low during this time of year, making it a popular time to visit the island. During the wet season, the weather is cooler and wetter, with frequent showers and thunderstorms. Temperatures range from 23 to 28 degrees Celsius during this time of year (Dominica Tourism Board, n.d.).

The climate crisis has had a significant impact on Dominica's climate and its ecosystems. The island has experienced an increase in the frequency and intensity of extreme weather events, such as hurricanes, floods, and landslides. These events have caused significant damage to the country's infrastructure and economy.

The climate crisis has also had an impact on the island's ecosystems. Corals and coral reefs have suffered significant damage due to rising water temperatures and ocean acidification. In addition, climate change has caused alterations in rainfall patterns, which has affected the island's biodiversity. Decreases in the population of some animal and plant species have been recorded, as well as an increase in the spread of invasive species (United Nations, 2019).

The Dominica government has taken steps to address the climate crisis and reduce the impacts on the country's climate and ecosystems. In 2017, Dominica pledged to be the first country in the world to become fully climate resilient. The government has adopted measures to increase energy efficiency, reduce greenhouse gas emissions and increase the country's adaptive capacity to the impacts of climate change (World Meteorological Organization, 2019).

# Tourist Attractions in Dominica

In this section, I will tell you in detail about all the tourist attractions in Dominica and all the possible activities you can do on this beautiful island.

Morne Trois Pitons National Park is one of the most popular parks in Dominica. It was declared a UNESCO World Heritage Site in 1997 due to its rich biodiversity and unique geological features. This park spans over 17,000 acres and features a variety of ecosystems, from tropical forests to crater lakes to hot springs. In addition, the park has numerous trails, waterfalls, rivers, and lakes, making it a paradise for nature lovers. Some of the most popular attractions in the park include Trafalgar Falls, Middleham Falls, Boiling Lake, and Boiling Volcano.

The Indian River Forest Reserve is a beautiful and peaceful place found on the north coast of Dominica. The river is home to a wide variety of birds and aquatic animals, and it is possible to take a guided riverboat tour to explore the area. During the tour, you can see the rich biodiversity of the river and the surrounding jungle.

Fort Shirley is a historical and cultural attraction in Dominica. It is an 18th-century fort located on the northwest coast of the island. The fort has been restored and is now a museum showcasing Dominica's history and culture. In addition, it is also possible to take a tour of the fort to learn more about its history.

The town of Kalinago is a native Caribbean village displaying the traditional way of life of the original inhabitants of the island. Visitors can learn about the culture and history of the Caribbean people and see how they live and work today.

The Papillote Botanical Garden has a wide variety of tropical plants and bird species. In addition, the garden features several thermal water pools, which are popular with visitors looking to relax and enjoy the natural beauty of the island.

The Museum of Dominica, located in the capital Roseau, is a fascinating place that houses a wide range of exhibits that highlight the history, culture, and biodiversity of the island. The museum has three main sections: the history section, covering everything from pre-Columbian times to Dominica's independence in 1978; the cultural section, which displays traditional artifacts and crafts from the island's indigenous and African peoples, as well as European and Asian influences; and the biodiversity section, which showcases the incredible variety of wildlife found on Dominica, which is known as "The Island of Nature." There is also a section dedicated to Dominica's music and carnival, where visitors can learn about the island's vibrant culture and traditions.

Dominica's Arawak Theater is a historic and iconic building located in the capital city of Roseau. Built in the 1950s, the theater has been the center of the island's cultural and artistic life for more than six decades. The theater can hold over 500 spectators and has been the site of a wide variety of performances, from operas and ballets to plays and live music concerts. The theater's architecture features a French Colonial style with a Caribbean twist, with high ceilings, wrought-iron balconies, and a bright green-painted façade. Today, the Arawak Theater remains a place of great cultural significance in Dominica and is the venue for some of the most prominent cultural events on the island.

The Dominica Caribbean Art Gallery is an institution dedicated to the promotion of Caribbean artists and the preservation of Caribbean culture through the exhibition of contemporary, traditional, and popular art. Founded in 1984, the gallery has an extensive collection of artwork by Caribbean artists, including paintings, sculptures, photographs, textiles, and ceramics. In addition to its permanent collection, the gallery organizes temporary exhibitions and cultural events, such as art workshops, talks, and traditional music and dance performances. The Dominica Caribbean Art Gallery also works in collaboration with other cultural institutions in the Caribbean and beyond to promote artistic and cultural dialogue and collaboration in the region.

This island paradise is known for having a large number of outdoor activities. One of the most popular activities is diving and snorkeling. The island has several coral reefs, allowing visitors to explore a wide variety of marine species, including tropical fish, corals, and turtles. Popular dive sites include Champagne Reef, located on the west coast of the island, and Scott's Head, located on the southern tip of the island.

In addition to diving and snorkeling, Dominica is ideal for hiking. The island has a large number of nature trails that allow visitors to explore the tropical jungle and mountainous landscapes. The most popular trail is the Waitukubuli National Trail, which runs the length of the island through 14 segments, offering stunning views of the ocean, rivers, and waterfalls.

For those seeking adventure, rafting, and kayaking are two exciting options. Dominica has several rivers, including the Layou River, which offers exciting rapids and beautiful views of the rainforest. Visitors can also rent kayaks and explore the island's coastline on their own.

In addition to these activities, Dominica also offers other outdoor options, such as bird watching, sport fishing, and exploring the island's waterfalls (Discover Dominica, 2022; Lonely Planet, 2022).

## Eco-Tourism

Dominica is known as the "Island of Nature" due to its stunning natural beauty and biological diversity. The island has a large number of ecotourism activities that allow visitors to explore and enjoy its rich biodiversity.

One of the most popular ecotourism activities in Dominica is hiking. The island has more than 300 miles of nature trails that traverse rainforests, mountains, and rivers. The most famous trail is the Waitukubuli National Trail, which offers stunning views of the mountainous landscape and the ocean. Visitors can walk on their own or join a local guide to learn about the local flora and fauna.

Another popular ecotourism activity is bird watching. Dominica is home to more than 200 species of birds, including the imperial parrot and the broad-winged petrel. Visitors can take a guided tour to watch birds in their natural habitat.

In addition to hiking and bird watching, Dominica offers other ecotourism activities, such as exploring waterfalls, diving and snorkeling in coral reefs, and visiting botanical gardens. Visitors can also enjoy kayaking through the island's rivers or whale and dolphin watching off the coast.

The island also has several conservation programs that allow visitors to learn more about protecting wildlife and the environment. One such program is the Imperial Parrot Conservation Project, which works to protect endangered species (Dominica National Parks and Wildlife Division, 2022; Discover Dominica, 2022; Lonely Planet, 2022).

# Accommodation

There is a wide variety of accommodation options in Dominica, from luxury hotels with ocean views to more affordable options such as apartments, hostels, and camping. In this article, we will explore the different accommodation options available in Dominica.

Luxury hotels in Dominica offer a unique lodging experience with stunning ocean views. These hotels are designed to provide guests with a luxurious and comfortable environment. Some of the most popular hotels include:

- **Secret Bay**: a luxury retreat located on the north coast of the island. It offers private villas with stunning sea views, private pools, and spa services.

- **Rosalie Bay Resort**: a luxury hotel located on the east coast of the island. It offers panoramic views of the Atlantic Ocean, a spa, a restaurant, and a variety of outdoor activities.

- **Jungle Bay Resort and Spa**: an ecological resort located on the south coast of the island. It offers bungalows with sea views, a spa, a restaurant, and outdoor activities.

If you are looking for cheaper options, several apartments and hotels offer affordable accommodation in Dominica. These hotels are ideal for travelers who want to enjoy the beauty of the island without spending a fortune. Some of the most popular hotels and apartments include:

- **Hibiscus Valley Inn**: a hotel located on the north coast of the island. It offers affordable rooms and bungalows surrounded by lush tropical vegetation.

- **The Champs**: A small boutique hotel located on the north coast of the island. It offers rooms with sea views, a swimming pool, and a restaurant.

- **Picard Beach Cottages**: a collection of cabins located on the north coast of the island. It offers affordable accommodation in picturesque and peaceful surroundings.

For travelers on a budget, hostels and campsites are excellent accommodation options. These places offer affordable accommodation in a relaxed and friendly environment. Some of the most popular hostels and campsites in Dominica include:

- **The Old Mill Cultural Center**: a hostel located on the west coast of the island. It offers affordable accommodation in a cultural and artistic environment.

- **Papillote Wilderness Retreat**: an eco-retreat located on the west coast of the island. It offers accommodation in cabins surrounded by nature and a natural spa.

- **Cabrits Resort & Spa Kempinski Dominica**: a luxury hotel located on the north coast of the island. It offers rooms with ocean views, a spa, a restaurant, and a variety of outdoor activities (TripAdvisor, 2022).

# Souvenirs Worth Buying

There are many souvenirs and souvenirs that tourists can buy to take home or give to loved ones. Here I present some ideas of gifts and souvenirs that you can find in Dominica:

- Local Art: Tourists can find beautiful pieces of local art that represent the culture of Dominica. They can be paintings, sculptures, and fabrics, among others. The paintings by the artist Isidore, for example, are very popular with tourists for their vibrant colors.

- Jewelry: Handmade jewelry is very popular in Dominica. Tourists can find unique pieces made with shells, stones, and local materials such as wood and seeds. The necklaces and bracelets made by the women of the Kalinago village are especially popular.

- Spices: Dominica is known for its spices and seasonings, such as capsicum, nutmeg, and ginger. Tourists can buy fresh and ground spices to take home and add to their meals.

- Clothing and Accessories: Tourists can find clothing and accessories made from local materials, such as cotton and linen. Tropical print dresses and shirts are very popular, as are bags and straw hats.

- Bath and beauty products: Tourists can find products made with local ingredients such as coconut oil, cocoa, and medicinal plants. Soaps and moisturizing creams are especially popular.

- Local Music: Music is an important part of Dominica's culture. Tourists can find CDs and vinyl by local reggae, calypso, and zouk artists.

- Books and Travel Guides: Tourists can purchase Dominica books and travel guides to learn more about the island's history, culture, and attractions (Caribbean & Co., 2021).

# Discovering Delicacies

The island also has a rich culinary tradition that combines African, French, and Caribbean influences. Dominica's typical dishes are a mix of flavors and textures that reflect the cultural diversity of the island.

One of the most popular dishes in Dominica is "calaloo," a vegetable stew made with taro leaves, okra, spinach, coconut, and meat. Fish is also very popular and can be found fresh in many of the island's restaurants. Other typical dishes include "saltfish," salted cod with onion, tomato, and pepper; "peas and rice," rice with peas and spices, and the "bouyon," a meat and vegetable stew.

The local fruits of Dominica are a delight. One of the most popular is the "marañón," also known as "breadfruit." This fruit is used in many dishes and can be eaten, cooked, roasted, or fried. Other local fruits include guava, mango, banana, and pineapple.

As for desserts, the island is famous for its yuca cakes, made with grated yucca, coconut, and sugar. It is also common to find fruit desserts such as "coconut tart," made with grated coconut, and "coconut flan," a coconut pudding and condensed milk.

Typical Dominica drinks include "coco punch," a drink made with rum, coconut milk, and spices; sorrel, a drink made with the flower of the hibiscus plant and spices; and ginger beer, a fizzy drink made with fresh ginger and lemon.

As far as the best restaurants and bars to visit on the island, there are plenty of great places to try some of Dominica's delicious food and drink. One of the most popular restaurants is "Old Stone Grill & Bar" in Roseau, which offers a variety of local dishes and fresh seafood. Another outstanding restaurant is "Papillote Wilderness Retreat" in Trafalgar, which serves local and international cuisine in a tropical setting.

For a more casual experience, many bars on the island offer drinks and casual dining. One of the most popular is the "Fort Young Hotel" in Roseau, which has a rooftop bar with stunning views of the city and the sea. Another popular venue is "Purple Turtle Beach Club" in Portsmouth, which offers live music and beachside drinks (Caribbean Journal, 2016; Discover Dominica, n.d.).

## Tips to Follow Before Visiting Dominica

Before visiting Dominica, there are some important things you should know regarding visas, entry conditions, health and safety, currency, and local language.

Citizens of some countries require a visa to enter Dominica. However, citizens of most countries can enter Dominica without a visa and stay for up to six months. Upon arrival in Dominica, visitors must present a valid passport and an exit ticket. If you plan to stay longer than six months, you will need to obtain a residence permit at the Immigration Office in Roseau.

Dominica has a good healthcare system, but visitors should take precautions to avoid illness. It is advisable to get vaccinated against typhoid fever, hepatitis A and B, and yellow fever if you are traveling from a country where these diseases are common. It is also important to take measures to prevent malaria and dengue, such as using insect repellent and protective clothing. Regarding security, visitors should be vigilant and take precautions in tourist areas and avoid certain areas at night.

Dominica's official currency is the East Caribbean dollar (XCD), which has a fixed exchange rate with the US dollar. Most businesses accept credit cards, but it is advisable to carry cash for small expenses and purchases in local markets. Dominica's official language is English, but French Creole is also spoken (Discover Dominica, 2022).

# Chapter 9: Roatán

Roatán is a beautiful island located in the Caribbean Sea, on the north coast of Honduras. It is the largest island of the Islas de la Bahía and is known for its stunning white sand beaches and crystal clear turquoise and deep blue waters. The island is also a paradise for lovers of diving and snorkeling, as it has one of the largest coral reefs in the world, full of colorful and fascinating marine life. In addition to its natural beauty, the island has a rich Garífuna history and culture, which is reflected in its music, dance, and cuisine.

## Location and How to Get There

Roatán is an island located in the Caribbean Sea, off the north coast of Honduras. It is located about 65 kilometers from the coast of La Ceiba, in the department of Atlántida, and about 55 kilometers north of the island of Utila. The island belongs to the Bay Islands, an archipelago consisting of three main islands: Roatán, Utila, and Guanaja, as well as several smaller islands.

To get to Roatán, there are several transportation options. The most common way to get there is by plane, through the Juan Manuel Gálvez International Airport, which is located in the town of Coxen Hole, on the west coast of the island. The airport receives national and international flights, mainly from airlines from North America, Central America, and the Caribbean. In addition, Roatán can be reached by ferry from La Ceiba, on the north coast of Honduras. The ferry leaves the port of La Ceiba several times a day and takes approximately two hours to reach the island.

The geographical location of Roatán is important for its economic and tourist development since it is located in a strategic position in the Caribbean Sea, which allows easy access to tourists from all over the world. In addition, the island has a warm and tropical climate throughout the year, which makes it an attractive tourist destination for lovers of the beach and the sea (Roatán Island Tourism Bureau, n.d.).

# Short History

The island of Roatán is located in the Islas de la Bahía archipelago in Honduras and is the largest of the islands. It was formed about 30 million years ago as part of a chain of seamounts that stretched from the mainland to what is now the Caribbean Sea. Over time, erosion and tectonic activity pushed these mountains out of the water, and the island emerged.

Over the centuries, the island has been home to various animal and plant species, many of which are endemic to the region. Among the animals that inhabited the island are various species of reptiles, including lizards, iguanas, and snakes. There were also birds, such as parrots and hummingbirds, and mammals such as monkeys, anteaters, and armadillos.

Fossil records have been found of a species of giant sloth called Megalonyx Jeffersonii, which inhabited the island more than 10,000 years ago, and this species is believed to be one of the main reasons the Garífuna settled on the island.

The Garífuna arrived on the island of Roatán about 2,000 years ago, after fleeing slavery in other parts of the Caribbean. It is believed that they settled in the region due to the presence of giant sloths, which provided an abundant food source.

The Garífuna brought with them their own culture and language, which is still preserved on the island today. The Garífuna culture is characterized by its music and dance, which have been declared the Intangible Cultural Heritage of Humanity by UNESCO.

During colonial times, the island of Roatán was the subject of disputes between Spain and Great Britain, until it was finally colonized by the British in the 18th century. The British established cotton and sugar cane plantations on the island, bringing African slaves to work on them.

After Honduran independence in 1821, the island became part of Honduran territory, but the presence of the British and their influence on the island's culture and economy continued for decades. In 1859, Honduras ceded the island to Great Britain in a treaty, but in 1860 the cession was revoked and Honduran sovereignty over the island was restored.

Today, the island of Roatán is a popular tourist destination thanks to its white sand beaches, coral reefs, and rich Garifuna culture. The island's economy is based on tourism, fishing, and agriculture, and it is in a strategic position as a gateway to the Caribbean.

Roatán is part of Honduras and its population is a diverse mix of Garífuna, mestizo, and expatriates from various countries, especially the United States and Canada. Although the island is a tourist area, there are still economic and social challenges for many of its inhabitants, especially in the communities further away from the tourist centers.

Honduran politics has historically been turbulent, and the island of Roatán has been no stranger to political conflict. However, in recent years work has been done to improve infrastructure and security on the island, which has contributed to the growth of tourism and foreign investment.

The history of the island of Roatán is a mixture of geology, culture, and political conflict. From its formation millions of years ago to its current use as a tourist destination, the island has seen a variety of animal and plant species, as well as diverse cultures and conquests. Currently, the island continues to evolve as part of Honduras and as a tourist destination in the Caribbean (Chamberlain, S., 2009; Parker, M., 2016).

# Culture and Language

Honduras is a Central American country that shares its culture with its neighbors to the north, south, and east, while Raotán is an island in the Gulf of Honduras that has developed its own culture over time. Both have a rich history and cultural heritage, which can be seen in their music, traditions, customs, and language.

Music in Honduras is varied and diverse, reflecting the influence of indigenous, African, and Spanish cultures. Traditional music includes Garífuna, folk music, merengue, cumbia, and salsa. Garífuna is a musical genre that originated on the north coast of Honduras and combines elements of African and Caribbean music. It is a very lively rhythm and is played with instruments such as drums, guitars, and maracas. On the other hand, folk music is a mixture of popular rhythms and songs, played on traditional instruments such as the guitar, violin, and marimba.

Regarding traditions, Honduras has a rich pre-Hispanic history that is reflected in its traditions and customs. One of the most important traditions is the celebration of the Day of the Dead, which is celebrated on November 2. During this festivity, families gather to honor their loved ones who have passed away, and altars are prepared with offerings and flowers. Processions and parades are also held in the streets.

In Raotán, traditions, and customs are also deeply rooted in the local culture. One of the most important celebrations is Holy Week, which is celebrated on the island every year. During this holiday, processions and parades are held in the streets, and religious ceremonies are held in the local church.

The official language of Honduras is Spanish, although other indigenous languages such as Garífuna and Miskito are also spoken. In Raotán, the official language is Spanish, although Creole English is also spoken. Creole English is spoken on the Caribbean coast of Honduras and is a mixture of English, Spanish, and African languages.

The official currency of Honduras is the lempira, named after the indigenous leader Lempira, who fought against the Spanish conquistadors in the 16th century. The coin was introduced in 1931 and has remained the official currency ever since. In Raotán, the lempira is also used as the official currency.

In addition to music, traditions, language, and currency, there are other interesting cultural aspects in Honduras and Raotán. For example, the gastronomy of Honduras is very varied and reflects the influence of indigenous, African, and Spanish cultures. Some of the most popular dishes include pupusas, tamales, and baleada. In Raotán, the cuisine focuses on fresh seafood and Creole dishes.

Honduras and Raotán have a rich and diverse culture that can be appreciated in their music, traditions, customs, language, and gastronomy. Although they share some similarities with neighboring Central American countries, they have developed their own cultural identity over time. Traditional music, such as Garífuna and folk music, is very lively and is played on traditional instruments. Traditions and customs, such as the celebration of the Day of the Dead in Honduras and Holy Week in Raotán, are very important to the local culture. Spanish is the official language in both places, although other indigenous and Creole languages are also spoken. The official currency of Honduras, the lempira, is named after an indigenous leader who fought against the Spanish conquistadors. In addition, the gastronomy of both places is very varied and reflects the influence of indigenous, African, and Spanish cultures (González, H., 2013; Linares, L., 2014).

## Weather and Climate

The climate in Roatán is influenced by the warm current of the Caribbean and the proximity of the continent, which means that the average annual temperature is 27 °C and the rains are abundant throughout the year.

The weather in Roatán is divided into two seasons: the dry season, which runs from February to July, and the rainy season, which runs from August to January. During the dry season, the humidity decreases and the days are sunnier and warmer, while during the rainy season, the humidity increases, and the rains can be torrential, especially in the months of October and November.

The impact of climate change on Roatán has become a matter of concern for the scientific community and the inhabitants of the island. The effects of climate change on Roatán are multiple and varied, including an increase in average air and sea temperatures, ocean acidification, loss of coral reefs, and intensification of extreme weather events.

According to the Intergovernmental Panel on Climate Change (IPCC), the average air temperature in the Caribbean region is expected to increase between 1.4 °C and 3.8 °C by the year 2100, which would have a significant impact on Roatan weather. In addition, the sea level is expected to rise, which could lead to flooding and damage to coastal infrastructure.

In terms of ecosystems, Roatán's coral reefs are particularly vulnerable to climate change due to rising sea temperatures and ocean acidification. Coral reefs are important for coastal protection, biodiversity, and tourism, which is an important source of income for the local economy. The loss of coral reefs would have a significant impact on the local economy and the region's marine biodiversity.

In conclusion, Roatán's climate is humid and warm tropical, with a dry season and a rainy season. Climate change is significantly affecting the island, with an increase in air and sea temperatures, acidification of the oceans, and the loss of coral reefs. It is important to take steps to reduce greenhouse gas emissions and protect Roatán's marine ecosystems to ensure their long-term sustainability (IPCC, 2014; Shantz, A. A., & Burkepile, D. E., 2014; Mumby, P. J., Hastings, A ., & Edwards, H.J., 2007).

# Tourist Attractions in Roatán

From its beautiful beaches to its natural parks, the island offers a wide variety of options to satisfy the tastes and needs of visitors.

One of the main tourist attractions in Roatán is its white sand beaches and crystal clear waters. Notable ones include West Bay Beach, Half Moon Bay, Sandy Bay Beach, and Mahogany Bay. These beaches are ideal for water sports such as snorkeling, diving, paddleboarding, kayaking, and sailing.

In addition to the beaches, Roatán has a large number of recreation places, ecological reserves, and natural parks. Gumbalimba Park, for example, is a nature reserve that has a wide variety of flora and fauna, including monkeys, parrots, and butterflies. Other popular natural parks include the Sandy Bay-West End National Park and the Cayos Cochinos National Park.

As for historical places and museums, Roatán has several interesting places to visit. One of the highlights is the Roatán Museum, located in the town of Coxen Hole, it offers a deeper look into the history and culture of the island. The museum has a variety of exhibits including indigenous artifacts, historical documents, and photographs of daily life on the island. It is also possible to visit the church of Santa Elena, built in 1875, and the Fuerte de la Concepción, a fortress built in the 18th century to protect the island from pirates.

The island was inhabited by the Paya Indians before the arrival of the Spanish in the 16th century. Later, the island became a strategic point for pirates and buccaneers, who used it as a base for their looting operations in the Caribbean Sea.

In the 18th century, the British settled on Roatán, and the island became a British colony. As a result, the island has a British cultural influence, which is reflected in its architecture, food, and customs.

The Roatán House of Culture is another interesting place to visit. The building was built in the 1920s and has become a center of culture and the arts on the island. The museum features a variety of exhibits that highlight Roatán's history and culture, including music, dance, cuisine, and visual arts.

The Fort of San Fernando, built in the 18th century, is another historical place on the island that is worth visiting. The fort was built to protect the island from pirate attacks and is one of the few places left from the British colonial days on the island.

When it comes to recreation, there are many exciting activities to choose from. Tourists can practice water sports such as diving, snorkeling, and kayaking. There are numerous dive companies on Roatán, such as Bananarama Dive Center, Subway Watersports, and Coconut Tree Divers, offering excursions and courses for beginners and experts alike.

Several companies offer tours around the island, such as Roatán Island Tours and Roatán Excursions. Tourists can visit places like the Sandy Bay National Park, the Carambola Botanical Garden, and the Gumbalimba Nature Reserve (Roatán Tourism Bureau, n.d.).

# Accommodation

There are a wide variety of lodging options available on Roatan, from luxury ocean-view hotels to more affordable options such as hostels and campgrounds.

Luxury hotels in Roatán offer a wide range of amenities for their guests, from luxury spas to gourmet restaurants. One of the most popular hotels in Roatán is the Mayan Princess Beach & Dive Resort, which has beautiful ocean-view rooms and a wide range of activities for guests, including scuba diving, kayaking, and boating. Another luxury hotel in Roatán is the Infinity Bay Spa & Beach Resort, which offers luxurious rooms, a full-service spa, and a gourmet restaurant.

For those looking for cheaper accommodation options, apartments, and cabins are popular choices. Roatán has a large number of apartments and cabins that can be rented for a reasonable price. These accommodations offer greater privacy and a more home-like atmosphere for guests. One of the most popular places to stay on Roatán is Blue Island Divers, which offers cabins and apartments in an ideal location, close to the beach and local tourist attractions.

Hostels and campgrounds are even cheaper lodging options for those looking to save money on their trip to Roatán. Roatan hostels are a popular choice for travelers who want to meet other travelers and enjoy a more relaxed atmosphere. One of the most popular hostels on Roatán is the Coconut Tree West End Hostel, which offers affordable accommodation in a central location on the island. For travelers who want to camp, Roatán has several campgrounds that offer beautiful views and a wide range of outdoor activities (Booking, 2023).

## Souvenirs Worth Buying

One of the most popular places to buy souvenirs is in the tourist area of West End, where there are numerous craft and souvenir shops. Among the options available are island-themed t-shirts, fridge magnets, mugs with images of the island, and hand-carved wooden crafts.

Another option to buy souvenirs in Roatán is visiting the island's markets, where you can find local products and crafts from area artisans. One of the most popular markets is the Coxen Hole Market, where you can find carved wooden objects, jewelry, pottery, and local clothing.

It is also possible to buy souvenirs and handicrafts in the local towns of Roatán, such as the town of Punta Gorda, where you can find unique pieces of handicrafts made by the local inhabitants. In this town, you can find ceramic objects, fabrics, and leather goods.

For those interested in purchasing luxury items, several unique stores on Roatán offer high-end jewelry, clothing, and other items. One of the most exclusive places is Diamonds International, a jewelry store that offers a wide variety of diamonds and other precious stones (Caribbean & Co., 2021).

## Discovering Delicacies

This precious Caribbean jewel has a wide variety of typical dishes, local fruits, drinks, and desserts that are part of its rich gastronomic culture. The island has a mixture of Spanish, African, and Caribbean influences, which have created a unique fusion of flavors and aromas.

One of the most traditional Roatán dishes is the "baleada," a kind of flour tortilla filled with beans, cheese, and cream. This dish is very popular on the island and can be found in many places, from street stalls to high-end restaurants.

Another very popular dish on Roatán is "sopa de caracol," a seafood soup with conch shells, plantains, and yucca. This soup is very tasty and nutritious and can be found in many local restaurants.

The "rice and beans" is another typical dish of the island, consisting of rice cooked with red beans and grated coconut. This dish is often served as a side to other main dishes, such as fried fish or roast chicken.

As for local fruits, Roatán has a wide variety, such as pineapple, mango, coconut, papaya, and guava. These fruits can be found in many places on the island, from the local markets to the fruit stalls on the beach.

Typical Roatán drinks include "horchata," a drink made from rice and cinnamon, and "agua de sapo," a drink made from ginger, lemon, and sugar. It is also common to find fresh tropical fruit juices, such as pineapple juice or passion fruit juice.

When it comes to desserts, one of the most popular on Roatán is "pan de coco," a sweet bread made with grated coconut and sugar. Another delicious dessert is "dulce de papaya," a sweet made from papaya cooked with sugar and spices (Roatan Tourism Bureau, n.d.).

## Tips to Follow Before Visiting Roatan

If you plan to visit this place, it is important to know certain considerations about visas, health and safety, local currency, legislation, and other important information for planning your trip:

- Visas: If you are a citizen of most countries in North America, Central America, and Europe, you will not need a visa to visit Roatán, as long as your stay is less than 90 days. However, it is important to check the specific requirements of your country before you travel. You can obtain more information about visa requirements on the website of the Honduran Embassy in your country (Embassy of Honduras in the United States, 2023).

- Health and Safety: It is important to take precautionary measures to maintain your health and safety while visiting Roatán. It is advisable to get vaccinated against hepatitis A and B, as well as against typhoid fever and rabies if you plan to be in contact with animals. It is also recommended to drink bottled water and avoid raw or undercooked foods to prevent gastrointestinal diseases. Regarding security, it is important to be careful with your belongings and avoid walking alone in areas with little traffic at night. You may want to check the US Department of State's travel advisories for up-to-date information on safety in Roatán.

- Local currency: The official currency of Honduras is the lempira, but many places in Roatán accept US dollars. However, you may get better prices if you pay with the local currency. It is also advisable to carry cash since not all shops and restaurants accept credit cards.

- Legislation: As in most countries, there are certain laws and regulations that you should be aware of while visiting Roatan. For example, the use and possession of illicit drugs are illegal and can result in serious legal consequences. It is also important to respect private property and stay away from restricted areas on the beaches.

# Chapter 10: Maldives

The Maldives is an archipelago of 26 atolls made up of more than 1,000 coral islands, located in the Indian Ocean, southwest of Sri Lanka. This world-renowned tourist destination is famous for its white-sand beaches, crystal-clear turquoise waters, and spectacular marine life, including sea turtles, sharks, and dolphins. The Maldives offers a unique experience for lovers of diving and snorkeling, as well as a wide variety of water activities such as paddle surfing, kayaking, and surfing. Luxury island resorts offer accommodation in private overwater villas and boast high-quality spa facilities and restaurants, making the Maldives an ideal place to enjoy an unforgettable vacation in a tropical paradise.

## Location

The Maldives Islands, officially known as the Republic of Maldives, are an island country located in the Indian Ocean, southwest of India and Sri Lanka. The archipelago is made up of 26 natural atolls and 1 artificial atoll, for a total of 1,192 islands, of which only 192 are inhabited.

The Maldives stretch over 90,000 square miles (233,000 km²) and have a maximum length of 500 miles (800 km) from north to south and a maximum width of 80 miles (130 km) from east to west. The country has a land area of approximately 115 square miles (298 km²), making it one of the smallest countries in the world.

The Maldives islands are located in the region of the Indian Ocean known as the Island Arc, which stretches from southern India to the eastern coast of Africa. The archipelago lies between latitudes 4° and 8° N and longitudes 73° and 78° E. Due to its location on the equator, the Maldives has a tropical climate with hot and humid temperatures throughout the year.

The Maldives is a popular destination for tourists due to its beautiful white sand beaches, crystal clear waters, and abundant marine life. Although the country is made up of numerous islands, only a few are open to tourism and many are exclusive to resort guests (Central Intelligence Agency, 2022).

# Short History

The Maldives Islands are an archipelago of 26 atolls located in the Indian Ocean, south of India and west of Sri Lanka. The country consists of more than 1,190 islands, of which around 200 are inhabited. The Maldives are known for their white sandy beaches, crystal clear waters, and rich underwater world, making them a popular tourist destination.

The history of the Maldives dates back more than 2 billion years when they were formed from underwater volcanoes. Over time, the islands have moved and evolved due to natural geological processes. The archipelago is located in an area of high seismic and volcanic activity, which has resulted in the formation of numerous islands over the centuries.

Before the arrival of humans, the Maldives were home to a wide variety of endemic species, including birds, reptiles, and mammals. However, the arrival of humans and their impact on the environment has led to the extinction of many of these species.

The first human populations are believed to have arrived in the Maldives in the 5th century BC. Throughout history, the Maldives has been inhabited by various communities, including Buddhists, Hindus, and Muslims. In the 12th century, Islam was introduced to the Maldives and has been the predominant religion in the country ever since.

For centuries, the Maldives was an important trade hub in the region, thanks to its strategic location on maritime trade routes. The people of the Maldives traded in products such as timber, coconuts, pearls, and ivory, and established trade relations with countries such as India, Sri Lanka, and China.

In the 16th century, the Maldives were colonized by the Portuguese, who established a presence in the archipelago for over a century. In the 17th century, the Dutch took control of the Maldives, but their presence was brief, and the Maldives regained their independence soon after.

In 1887, the Maldives became a British protectorate, which meant Britain was in charge of the country's defense and foreign policy. However, the Maldives maintained a degree of autonomy in its internal government. In 1965, the Maldives became an independent country.

Today, the Maldives is a presidential republic with an economy based on tourism and fishing. The local currency is the Maldivian rupee and the majority of the population practices Islam. The Maldives is known to be one of the countries most vulnerable to climate change, with much of the country lying less than one meter above sea level.

In political terms, the country has experienced ups and downs in recent decades. In 2018, President Ibrahim Mohamed Sol was re-elected in controversial elections that were questioned by the opposition and the international community. Since then, the government has taken steps to restrict press freedom and has been criticized for human rights violations.

Despite these challenges, the Maldives remain a popular destination for tourism and are working to develop the tourism industry sustainably. The country has also set ambitious goals to reduce carbon emissions and protect the environment and has been an active advocate in international efforts to combat climate change (World Wildlife Fund, n.d.; BBC News, 2023).

# Culture and Language

The culture of the Maldives is rich and diverse, influenced by its geographical location in the Indian Ocean and by its long history of trade and colonization. The official language is Divehi, an Indo-Aryan language written with a variant of the Arabic alphabet.

Traditions and customs in the Maldives are largely influenced by Islam, the country's predominant religion. Religious practices are an integral part of daily life and the holy month of Ramadan is especially important to the

Maldivians. During this time, people fast during the day and gather to share meals with family and friends after sunset.

The Maldivians also celebrate various festivals and holidays throughout the year. Independence Day celebrated on July 26, is a major event commemorating the independence of the Maldives from British colonization in 1965. National Day of the Maldives, celebrated on January 1, is another important holiday that includes parades, speeches, and cultural events.

Music and dance are also integral parts of the Maldivian culture. Traditional Maldivian music, known as bodu beru, is a form of percussion played on large drums made from coconut logs. The traditional dance is called dhandi jehun, which consists of smooth, flowing movements and is performed on special occasions such as weddings and festivals.

The colonial influence on Maldivian culture is evident in the country's architecture and cuisine. The British colonized the Maldives for nearly a century, leaving their mark on colonial architecture and the custom of afternoon tea. Maldivian cuisine is characterized as spicy and aromatic and has been influenced by Indian, Asian, and Arabic cuisine (Visit Maldives, n.d.; Experience Travel Group, 2021).

# Weather and Climate

The climate of the Maldives is mainly influenced by its geographical location in the Indian Ocean and its topography made up of coral atolls. The climate is warm and tropical, with constant temperatures throughout the year.

The climate of the Maldives is divided into two seasons: the rainy season and the dry season. The rainy season generally runs from May to November, while the dry season occurs from December to April. During the rainy season, the islands experience heavy rain and strong winds, while the dry season is characterized by sunny days and clear skies.

Temperatures in the Maldives vary little throughout the year, with an average annual temperature of around 30 degrees Celsius. The maximum temperatures generally oscillate between 31 and 33 degrees Celsius, while the minimum is around 25 degrees Celsius. Humidity on the islands is high throughout the year, making the wind chill higher than the thermometer indicates.

The Maldives is in a zone of cyclonic activity, so during the rainy season, they can experience tropical cyclones and typhoons. These weather events can cause strong winds and heavy rain that can cause flooding and damage to local infrastructure.

Climate change has had a significant impact on the climate of the Maldives. Sea level rise has affected coral atolls, which are particularly vulnerable to erosion and ocean acidification. Additionally, rising water temperatures have caused coral bleaching and the death of marine life in the area. This has negatively affected tourism, one of the country's main sources of income (Wanderlust Magazine, 2021).

# Tourist Attractions in the Maldives

Maldives' tourist attractions mainly include its stunning white sand beaches, crystal clear waters, and perfect tropical climate. In addition, there are some historical places and ecological reserves that are also worth a visit.

One of the most popular attractions in the Maldives are the beaches, and some of the most popular include Bikini Beach on Rasdhoo Island, Maafushi Beach, Fihalhohi Beach, and Ukulhas Beach. These beaches offer white sand and crystal clear waters to relax and enjoy the sun. You can also do a large number of water activities such as diving, snorkeling, surfing, and motor boating.

Another of Maldives' tourist attractions is the Baa Ecological Reserve, which is one of the largest marine conservation areas in the world and is located in the north of the archipelago. This reserve is home to a wide variety of species of marine life, including whale sharks, sea turtles, and dolphins. Tourists can enjoy diving and snorkeling excursions to discover the biodiversity of the area.

As for historical sites, one of the most famous is the Maldives Religious and Cultural Center in the capital Malé. This center is housed in a 17th-century mosque and showcases Maldivian culture and religion through its artifacts and exhibits. Also in the capital is the Sultan Park Palace, which was built in the 17th century and is a fine example of traditional Maldivian architecture.

Lastly, you can also visit Ari Atoll, which is located in the western Maldives and is known for its amazing marine life and for being a great place for snorkeling and scuba diving. Several islands in the atoll offer a sustainable tourism experience, with accommodation in guest houses run by the local community.

# Accommodation

The Maldives are known for their beautiful beaches, crystal clear waters, and luxury resorts that offer a unique experience of staying in a tropical paradise. There is a wide variety of Maldives accommodation options to suit different budgets and traveler preferences.

The most luxurious and highly rated hotels in the Maldives are the five-star resorts, offering an unparalleled luxury experience with private overwater villas, private pools, world-class spas, and a myriad of activities and excursions. Some of the most famous resorts are Soneva Fushi, COMO Maalifushi, and Four Seasons Resort Maldives at Landaa Giraavaru. These resorts are ideal for couples and families looking for a romantic getaway or a relaxing vacation in luxurious surroundings.

For those looking for a more modest option, the Maldives also has modern and country-style cottages, inns, and apartments. These accommodations are ideal for travelers looking for a more authentic and local Maldivian experience, and who prefer to avoid the tourist resorts. Some of the most popular accommodations are Fulidhoo La Perla Guest House, Crystal Sands Beach Hotel, and Summer Villa Guest House.

In addition, there are a wide variety of hostels and campsites in the Maldives, which are ideal for backpackers and travelers looking for a more affordable accommodation option. Hostels offer shared and private rooms, and some even have dormitory options on the terraces of the cabins. Some of the most popular hostels are the Central View Guesthouse, the Relax Beach Inn, and the Himandhoo Inn (Visit Maldives, 2021).

# Souvenirs Worth Buying

The Maldives is an idyllic place to enjoy a dream vacation. This archipelago of islands is known for its white sand beaches, crystal clear waters, and multicolored corals, making it a very popular tourist destination. Apart from the natural beauty, the Maldives also has a lot to offer in terms of souvenirs and gifts to remember your experience in this place.

One of the most popular options is artistic pieces. The Maldivians are known for their skill in making handicrafts such as wood carvings, weaving, and palm baskets. These pieces are unique and reflect local culture and tradition. An example of this is the hammerhead shark wood carving, a species that is very common in these waters. These carvings are handmade and are a sample of local artwork.

Another option that can serve as a gift or souvenir is traditional liquors or drinks. The most popular drink in the Maldives is raa, an alcoholic drink made from coconut palm. This drink is very popular among the local inhabitants and can be found in any market in the city. In addition, the raa is also used in the preparation of local dishes such as garudhiya, a fish broth.

Local sweets are also a popular option to take home as a souvenir or gift. One of the most popular sweets is huni hakuru, made with coconut and palm molasses. Another popular sweet is bondibai, a dessert made with rice and shredded coconut.

Finally, many other souvenir options can remember your vacation in the Maldives. You can find everything from t-shirts and mugs with local designs, to jewelry and personal care products made with natural ingredients from the region (Visit Maldives, 2021).

# Discovering Delicacies

Maldivian food is known for its freshness and marine flavor, using mainly local ingredients and exotic spices.

One of the most iconic Maldivian dishes is Mas Huni, a breakfast dish made from fresh tuna, onion, grated coconut, and chili. Another popular dish is Garudhiya, a fish soup with rice and lemon, which is served in most Maldivian homes and restaurants.

Local fruits include coconut, papaya, mango, and banana. These fruits are commonly used in the preparation of desserts and typical drinks. In addition, bananas are also widely used to prepare Kashikeyo Bai, a dish made with rice and banana that is steamed.

As for alcoholic beverages, the most popular is Raa, a local liquor made from fermented coconut palm. Imported beers and wines can also be found in most Maldivian bars and restaurants.

To try the typical Maldivian dishes, there are several recommended restaurants in the archipelago. One of them is the Ithaa Undersea Restaurant, a luxury underwater restaurant located in the Conrad Maldives Rangali Island complex, which offers a unique experience of tasting fresh seafood dishes while observing marine life.

Another recommended restaurant is Muraka, also located in the Conrad Maldives Rangali Island complex, which offers an exclusive and private dining experience in an underwater villa.

Finally, The Seagull Café restaurant is a popular option to try local food in a more casual and relaxed environment (Maldivian Cuisine, n.d.).

# Tips to Follow Before Visiting the Maldives

The Maldives is a very popular tourist destination that offers a host of attractions for all visitors, from paradisiacal beaches to water sports and a unique and fascinating culture. If you are planning to visit this island country, there are a few things you should know before your trip to ensure you have a safe and unforgettable experience.

Visitors from most countries do not need a visa to enter the Maldives. However, citizens of some countries, such as India and China, need to obtain a visa before they travel. If you are not sure whether you need a visa, it is best to check with the Maldivian embassy in your country before making your travel plans.

There are no mandatory vaccination requirements to enter the Maldives, however, it is advisable to be up to date with common vaccinations such as Hepatitis A and B, Tetanus, and Typhoid. Also, travelers are advised to bring insect repellent and sunscreen, as there is a high probability of mosquito bites and sun exposure is very intense.

The Maldives is a safe country for visitors, but like anywhere else, it's important to take basic security measures to ensure a smooth trip. Tourists are advised to avoid carrying large sums of cash and to keep an eye on their belongings at all times, especially in crowded areas.

Recommended vaccinations include hepatitis A and B, tetanus, and typhoid. The flu vaccine is also recommended for those traveling during the flu season.

The official currency of the Maldives is the Maldivian rupee, but the US dollar and Euro are also widely accepted in most tourist locations. The official language is Dhivehi, but English is widely spoken in tourist areas.

Islam is the official religion of the Maldives and is an important part of the daily life of the inhabitants of the country. Visitors should be respectful of local customs and traditions, such as dressing modestly when visiting religious sites and refraining from drinking alcohol in public (Maldives Embassy, 2022; Centers for Disease Control and Prevention, 2021; U.S. Department of State; 2022).

# Conclusion

Exploring the ten most paradisiacal islands in the world is a dream that many travelers have. Each of these islands has its own personality and charm, allowing you to connect with the nature, history, and culture of each place. If you are looking for a place to escape from the daily grind, these islands may be the perfect solution.

Curaçao is one of the most vibrant and colorful islands in the Caribbean region. With its crystal clear water, white sand beaches, and brightly painted houses, Curaçao is a true paradise for lovers of nature and culture. If you're looking for a cultural immersion experience, don't miss Willemstad's Old Town, with its Dutch colonial architecture and lively restaurants and bars.

The Bahamas, on the other hand, is a classic destination for those looking for a luxurious escape in the Caribbean. With its crystal clear waters and white sand beaches, the Bahamas is an ideal destination for those seeking peace and tranquility in luxurious surroundings. But not everything is about relaxation in the Bahamas, you can also enjoy a wide variety of water activities, such as diving, snorkeling, or paddle boarding.

Martinique is a French island in the Caribbean that attracts travelers with its unique blend of French and Caribbean influences. The island boasts a variety of landscapes, from white sand beaches to waterfalls and mountains. The capital city, Fort-de-France, is a true cultural treasure, with its streets lined with shops, restaurants, and bars.

Barbados is another Caribbean island that will take your breath away. Home to some of the best resorts in the Caribbean, Barbados is the perfect place for a romantic getaway or honeymoon. But Barbados also has a rich history and culture to explore, such as the St. Nicholas Abbey Sugar Plantation, a National Historic Landmark that dates back to the 17th century.

Saint Kitts is a small Caribbean island that offers much more than its size might suggest. With its myriad of historical sites, including Brimstone Hill Fortress, a UNESCO World Heritage Site, Saint Kitts is an ideal island for those who want to explore the history and culture of the Caribbean.

Negril, Jamaica is another popular destination for lovers of the sun and the beach. With its miles of white sand beaches and crystal clear waters, Negril is an ideal place to relax and enjoy the sun and sea. But if you are looking for something more active, you can also practice water sports such as snorkeling, windsurfing, and kitesurfing.

Puerto Rico is a destination that has something for everyone. With its unique blend of Spanish, African, and Taino influences, Puerto Rico is a melting pot of cultures and an ideal place to explore the history and culture of the Caribbean. But Puerto Rico also has some of the best beaches in the Caribbean, like Playa Flamenco on the island of Culebra, which has been voted one of the best beaches in the world.

Dominica is an island in the Caribbean less known than others, but no less beautiful. Known as the "Island of Nature," Dominica has an abundance of hiking trails and waterfalls to explore. It is also a great place for snorkeling and diving, with an abundance of marine life to discover in its crystal clear waters.

Roatán, in Honduras, is an island that combines natural beauty with a host of activities for visitors. The island is home to a large number of coral reefs, making it an ideal destination for diving and snorkeling. But Roatán also has a host of land-based attractions, such as the Roatán Butterfly Garden, where you can see dozens of different species of butterflies.

Last but not least is the Maldives, a chain of islands located in the Indian Ocean. With its crystal clear water and diverse marine life, the Maldives is a paradise for lovers of diving and snorkeling. But the Maldives also offers a wealth of luxury resort options, making them an ideal destination for a romantic or luxury getaway.

In conclusion, traveling to any of these ten paradise islands can be an enriching experience. In addition to enjoying the sun and the beach, you can connect with nature, explore local history and culture, and immerse yourself in the rich mix of cultural and culinary influences that characterize each of these islands.

Traveling is also a way of personal enrichment, learning about new cultures and ways of life, and opening our minds and hearts to new experiences and perspectives. If you are looking for a place to escape daily stress, relax and recharge your batteries, or simply live a unique and enriching experience, planning a trip to one of these ten paradisiacal islands is a great option.

No matter which of these ten islands you choose, one thing is sure: you will have unforgettable memories and unique experiences that you will remember forever. So why not start planning your next trip right now? There's a world full of adventure and discovery to discover, and these ten island paradises are just the beginning. Dare to explore and have the adventure of your life!

# Glossary

- **Cenozoic era**: The Cenozoic era is a geological era that began approximately 66 million years ago and continues to the present day. It is divided into three periods: the Paleogene, the Neogene, and the Quaternary. The Cenozoic era is known for the diversification of mammals and the rise of humans (University of California: Museum of Paleontology, n.d.).

- **Cretaceous period**: The Cretaceous period was the last period of the Mesozoic Era, lasting from approximately 145 to 66 million years ago. It is known for the proliferation of dinosaurs, including the Tyrannosaurus Rex and Triceratops, and the emergence of flowering plants (Science Learning Hub, n.d.).

- **Dialect**: A dialect is a form of language spoken in a specific region or community, characterized by unique vocabulary, grammar, and pronunciation. Dialects can vary greatly within a language and can often be influenced by historical, social, and cultural factors.

- **Ecologic reserve**: An ecological reserve is a protected area established to preserve and protect natural ecosystems and their biodiversity. These areas are often managed by governments or conservation organizations and can be used for scientific research, environmental education, and ecotourism.

- **Eco-tourism**: Eco-tourism is a type of sustainable tourism that aims to minimize the negative impact on the environment while providing visitors with educational and enjoyable experiences. This type of tourism focuses on natural and cultural heritage and often involves activities such as hiking, wildlife watching, and cultural tours (The International Ecotourism Society, 2015).

- **Eocene epoch**: The Eocene epoch is a geological epoch that lasted from approximately 56 to 33.9 million years ago, during the early part of the Cenozoic era. It is characterized by a global temperature increase, the emergence of new mammal and bird species, and the expansion of tropical forests (Science Learning Hub, n.d.).

- **Ice age**: An ice age is a period of geological history characterized by the presence of extensive continental glaciers and colder global temperatures. During an ice age, large portions of the earth's surface can be covered in ice, causing sea levels to drop and drastically changing landscapes and ecosystems (Encyclopaedia Britannica, n.d.).

- **Igneous rock**: Igneous rock is a type of rock that forms when magma or lava cools and solidifies. Igneous rocks can be intrusive (formed beneath the earth's surface) or extrusive (formed above the earth's surface) and are often characterized by their crystal size and texture (Geology, n.d.)

- **Island**: An island is a piece of land surrounded by water, smaller than a continent, and can be either formed by volcanic activity or separated from the mainland by a body of water.

- **Island tourism**: Island tourism refers to the travel industry centered around islands, which can offer unique natural landscapes, cultural experiences, and recreational activities. This type of tourism can range from luxurious resorts to eco-tourism, depending on the destination and traveler's interests.

- **National park**: A national park is a protected area designated by a government to preserve and protect unique natural landscapes and wildlife. These areas are often open to the public for recreational activities such as hiking, camping, and wildlife watching (National Park Service, 2022).

- **Tectonic plate**: A tectonic plate is a large slab of solid rock that makes up the earth's lithosphere, which is broken into several pieces that move relative to each other. Tectonic plates can collide, pull apart, or slide past each other, causing geological events such as earthquakes, volcanic eruptions, and the formation of mountains (National Geographic Society, 2022).

- **Tradition**: Tradition refers to customs, beliefs, and practices passed down from generation to generation within a culture or community.

These can include religious rituals, festivals, food, clothing, and other cultural practices.

- **Visa**: A visa is an official document that grants a person permission to enter and stay in a foreign country for a specific period. The type and duration of a visa can vary depending on the country, the purpose of travel, and the traveler's nationality.

# References

Acoya Curaçao Resort, Villas and Spa. (2019, August 7). *8 Things You Should Know Before Traveling to Curaçao*. Acoya Curaçao Resort, Villas and Spa. https://www.acoyaCuraçao.com/blog/8-Things-You-Should-Know-Before-Traveling-to-Curaçao

Airbnb. (n.d.). *Puerto Rico Vacation Rentals & Homes*. Airbnb. https://www.airbnb.com.ar/s/Puerto-Rico/homes?tab_id=home_tab&refinement_paths%5B%5D=%2Fhomes&flexible_trip_lengths%5B%5D=one_week&price_filter_input_type=0&price_filter_num_nights=5&query=Puerto%20Rico%2C%20Estados%20Unidos&place_id=ChIJ-aeSGyaWAowRGpsEGCjsNvM&date_picker_type=calendar&source=structured_search_input_header&search_type=autocomplete_click

Bahamas Food Tours. (n.d.). *The Importance of Bahamian Food*. Bahamasfoodtours.com. https://www.bahamasfoodtours.com/blog/the-importance-of-bahamian-food

Bahamas Handprints. (n.d.). *Shop*. Bahamahandprints.com. https://bahamahandprints.com/shop/

Bahamas Ministry of Tourism & Aviation. (n.d.). *Cuisine*. Bahamas.com. https://www.bahamas.com/es/article/cuisine-bahamas

Barbados Tourism Marketing Inc. (n.d.). *Barbados Climate*. Visit Barbados. https://www.visitbarbados.org/barbados-climate

Barbados Tourism Marketing Inc. (n.d.). *Culture*. Visit Barbados. https://www.barbados.org/culture.htm

Barbados Tourism Marketing Inc. (n.d.). *Departure Tax*. Visit Barbados. https://www.gobarbados.org/departure-tax.htm

Barbados Tourism Marketing Inc. (n.d.). *History of Barbados*. Visit Barbados. https://www.visitbarbados.org/about-barbados/history-of-barbados

Barbados Tourism Marketing Inc. (n.d.). *Where to Stay*. Visit Barbados. https://www.visitbarbados.org/where-to-stay

BBC News. (2011, March 8). *Maldives country profile*. BBC News. https://www.bbc.com/news/world-south-asia-12651486

Best Location Hotels. (n.d.). *Curaçao Hotels: Find the Best Hotels & Places to Stay*. Best Location Hotels. https://bestlocationhotels.com/destination/Curaçao/

Booking.com. (n.d.). *Roatan Island, Honduras*. Booking.com. https://www.booking.com/searchresults.es-ar.html?ss=Roatan+Island%2C+Honduras&efdco=1&label=gen173nr-1BCAEoggI46AdIM1gEaAyIAQGYASy4ARfIAQzYAQHoAQGIAgGoAgO4Aqqjo6AGwAIBogIkYjM2NmYoM2QtNDZiYSooNWI3LWJkN2UtMTA4YjUwZGJmZjBi2AIF4AIB&sid=d300857633f69186e8804fbac041ede8&aid=304142&lang=es-ar&sb=1&src_elem=sb&src=index&dest_id=6086&dest_type=region&ac_position=0&ac_click_type=b&ac_langcode=en&ac_suggestion_list_length=5&search_selected=true&search_pageview_id=41548od5bfe8096d&ac_meta=GhAoMTUoODBkNWJmZTgwOTZkIAAoATICZW46BnJvYXRhbkAASgBQAA%3D%3D&group_adults=2&no_rooms=1&group_children=0&sb_travel_purpose=leisure

Britannica. (n.d.). *Culture of Dominica*. Encyclopædia Britannica. https://www.britannica.com/place/Dominica/Culture

Britannica. (n.d.). *Curaçao*. Encyclopedia Britannica. https://www.britannica.com/place/Curaçao

Britannica. (n.d.). *Dominica*. Encyclopædia Britannica. https://www.britannica.com/place/Dominica

Bucket List Journey. (2022, February 10). *50+ Best Things to Do in the Bahamas*. Bucket List Journey. https://bucketlistjourney.net/bahamas-bucket-list-best-things-to-do/

Caribbean & Co. (2019, February 6). *10 authentic souvenirs to buy in Dominica*. Caribbean & Co. https://www.caribbeanandco.com/dominica-souvenirs/

Caribbean & Co. (2022, March 5). *Roatan Shopping Guide: 10+ Local Souvenirs & Unique Gifts*. Caribbean & Co. https://www.caribbeanandco.com/roatan-shopping-guide-local-souvenirs-unique-gifts/

Caribbean Journal. (2016, November 23). *10 must-eat dishes in Dominica*. Caribbean Journal. https://www.caribjournal.com/2016/11/23/10-must-eat-dishes-in-dominica/

Carnival Cruise Line. (n.d.). *10 Amazing Things to Buy When You're in the Bahamas*. Carnival.com. https://www.carnival.com/awaywego/travel/bahamas/10-amazing-things-to-buy-when-youre-in-the-bahamas

Carnival Cruise Line. (n.d.). *8 Best Things to Buy in Curaçao*. Carnival Cruise Line. https://www.carnival.com/awaywego/travel/caribbean/8-best-things-to-buy-in-Curaçao

Carnival Cruise Line. (n.d.). *Top 10 Things to Eat in Curaçao*. Carnival Cruise Line. https://www.carnival.com/awaywego/travel/caribbean/top-10-things-to-eat-in-Curaçao

Carry On Chronicles. (n.d.). *Best Areas to Stay in Curaçao*. Carry On Chronicles. https://www.carryonchronicles.com/best-areas-to-stay-in-Curaçao/

Centers for Disease Control and Prevention. (n.d.). *Health Information for Travelers to The Bahamas*. Cdc.gov. https://wwwnc.cdc.gov/travel/notices/watch/vaccinations

Centers for Disease Control and Prevention. (n.d.). *Maldives. Travelers' Health*. https://wwwnc.cdc.gov/travel/destinations/traveler/none/maldives

Central Intelligence Agency. (2022, February 28). *Maldives*. The World Factbook. Central Intelligence Agency. https://www.cia.gov/the-world-factbook/countries/maldives/

Chamberlain, S. (2009). *Roatán: A History of the Bay Islands and the Island of Roatán, Honduras*. Honduran Emeralds, LLC.

Christoffel National Park. (n.d.). *Explore the Park.* https://Curaçao.com/en/directory/do/christoffel-national-park/

Crask, P. (2014). *Dominica: Island Guide.*

Curaçao.com. (n.d.). *Guides to Curaçao.* Curaçao.com. https://Curaçao.com/en/directory/travel-guides/

Curaçao Maritime. (n.d.). *About us.* https://www.Curaçaomaritime.com/about-us/

Curaçao Tourist Board. (n.d.). *Celebrations & events.* https://www.Curaçao.com/en/celebrations-and-events/

Curaçao Tourist Board. (n.d.). *Fort Amsterdam.* https://Curaçao.com/en/directory/do/fort-amsterdam/

Curaçao Tourist Board. (n.d.). *Grote Knip.* https://Curaçao.com/en/directory/do/grote-knip/

Curaçao Tourist Board. (n.d.). *Mambo Beach Boulevard.* https://Curaçao.com/en/directory/do/mambo-beach-boulevard/

Dana Berez. (n.d.). *Curaçao Island Guide: Everything You Need to Know.* Dana Berez. https://danaberez.com/Curaçao-island/

De La Fuente, S. (2010). *Island Biogeography in the Caribbean.* University of Chicago Press.

Discover Dominica Authority. (n.d.). *Culture & Traditions.* Discover Dominica. https://discoverdominica.com/en/culture-traditions

Discover Dominica Authority. (n.d.). *Experiences.* Discover Dominica. https://discoverdominica.com/en/experiences

Discover Dominica Authority. (n.d.). *Restaurants.* Discover Dominica Authority. https://discoverdominica.com/restaurants

Discover Puerto Rico. (n.d.). *Cueva del Indio.* Discover Puerto Rico. https://www.discoverpuertorico.com/profile/cueva-del-indio/8941

Discover Puerto Rico. (n.d.). *Important Information.* Discover Puerto Rico. https://www.discoverpuertorico.com/es/travel-information/important-information

Dominica. (n.d.). *Plan your trip*. Discover Dominica Authority. https://dominica.dm/tourism/planyourtrip/

Dominica Welcome. (n.d.). *Climate*. Dominica Welcome. https://dominicawelcome.com/es/clima/

Dracius, S. (1998). *Flamboyère, suivi de L'Epître à la Terre Charnelle.*

Dubelaar, C. N. (2001). A History of Race Relations in Martinique: The Curious Case of a Dutch Anthropologist in the French Caribbean. *Small Axe, 5*(2), 128-146. https://doi.org/10.1215/07990537-5-2-128

Embassy of The Bahamas. (n.d.). *About The Bahamas*. Embassy of The Bahamas. https://www.bahamasembdc.org/about-the-bahamas/

Embassy of the Republic of Maldives, New Delhi. (n.d.). *Visa Information*. Maldivesembassy.in. https://maldivesembassy.in/visa-information/

Emerson, R. W. (1903). *Essays: First and second series*. P. F. Collier & Son.

Encyclopædia Britannica. (n.d.). *Barbados*. Encyclopædia Britannica. https://www.britannica.com/place/Barbados

Encyclopædia Britannica. (n.d.). *Ice Age*. Encyclopædia Britannica. https://www.britannica.com/science/ice-age

Encyclopædia Britannica. (n.d.). *Jamaica*. Encyclopædia Britannica. https://www.britannica.com/place/Jamaica/History

Encyclopædia Britannica. (n.d.). *The Bahamas*. Encyclopædia Britannica. https://www.britannica.com/place/The-Bahamas

Encyclopedia of Puerto Rico. (n.d.). *Cueva del Indio*. Encyclopedia of Puerto Rico. https://enciclopediapr.org/en/encyclopedia/cueva-del-indio/

Experience Travel Group. (2021, June 2). *Maldives Culture: Local Life, Traditions and Beliefs*. Experience Travel Group. http://www.experiencetravelgroup.com/blog/2021/06/maldives-culture/

Geology. (n.d.). *Igneous Rocks*. Geology. https://geology.com/rocks/igneous-rocks/

Ghasemi, A., Kheirkhah, M., & Roushani, E. (2019). Geological and hydrological features of the karst system of the northern coast of Puerto Rico. *Journal of African Earth Sciences, 150*, 182-193. https://doi.org/10.1016/j.jafrearsci.2019.01.013

González, H. (2013). El Garífuna: música y cultura de Honduras. *Nómadas, (38)*, 74-85.

Google Maps. (n.d.). *Dominica.* Google Maps. https://www.google.com/maps/place/Dominica/@14.9713783,-63.2689347,6.42z/data=!4m6!3m5!1s0x8c14d2faf2155a15:0x49b391 09053afd3c!8m2!3d15.414999!4d-61.370976!16zL20vMDI3bmI

Google Maps. (n.d.). *Martinique.* https://www.google.com/maps/place/Martinique/@14.6571161,-61.0582687,9z/data=!4m5!3m4!1s0x8c12bb027e8c545b:0x406aa0! 8m2!3d14.6415292!4d-61.0241744

Government of the Commonwealth of Dominica. (n.d.). *Wildlife Conservation.* Ministry of Environment, Climate Resilience, Disaster Management, and Urban Renewal. https://www.dominica.gov.dm/environment/national-parks/management/wildlife-conservation

Honychurch, L. (1995). *The Dominica Story: A History of the Island.*

Hughes, L. (1997). *The Collected Poems of Langston Hughes.* Knopf.

In Search of Sarah. (n.d.). *Curaçao Travel Tips - What to Know Before You Go.* In Search of Sarah. https://insearchofsarah.com/Curaçao-travel-tips/

IPCC. (2014). *Climate change 2014: Impacts, adaptation and vulnerability.* Contribution of Working Group II to the Fifth Assessment Report of the Intergovernmental Panel on Climate Change. Cambridge University Press.

IUCN Red List of Threatened Species. (n.d.). *Search.* https://www.iucnredlist.org/search

Koster, H. (1999). *The Dutch in the Caribbean and in the Guianas 1680-1791.* University of Michigan Press.

Linares, L. (2014). Cultura e identidad de los hondureños. *Revista de Ciencias Sociales,* (4), 143-154.

Lonely Planet. (n.d.). *Culture - Martinique.* Lonelyplanet.com. https://www.lonelyplanet.com/martinique/background/culture

Lonely Planet. (n.d.). *Outdoor activities in Dominica.* Lonely Planet. https://www.lonelyplanet.com/dominica/outdoor-activities

Loop News. (2020, October 14). *10 things to know before going to Curaçao.* Loop News. https://tt.loopnews.com/content/10-things-know-going-Curaçao

Martinique Tourism Authority. (n.d.). *Culinary Specialties.* Martinique Tourism Authority. https://us.martinique.org/discover/culinary-specialties

Martinique Tourism Authority. (n.d.). *La Martinique en quelques mots.* Martinique.org. https://www.martinique.org/la-martinique-en-quelques-mots/

Martinique Tourism Authority. (n.d.). *Martinique Island.* Martinique Tourism Authority. https://www.martinique.org/en/

Mikve Israel-Emanuel Synagogue. (n.d.). *Visit Us.* https://Curaçao.com/en/directory/do/mikve-israel-emanuel-synagogue/

Ministry of Economic Development, Curaçao. (2014). *Sustainable Development in Curaçao: The Way Forward.* https://ser.cw/wp-content/uploads/2015/09/Sustainable-Development-in-Cura%C3%A7ao-The-Way-Forward-2014.pdf

Ministry of Foreign Affairs, The Bahamas. (n.d.). *About The Bahamas. Ministry of Foreign Affairs.* The Bahamas. https://mofa.gov.bs/about-the-bahamas/

Ministry of Foreign Affairs. (n.d.). *Entry Requirements.* Mofa.gov.bs. https://mofa.gov.bs/entry-requirements/

Mumby, P. J., Hastings, A., & Edwards, H. J. (2007). Thresholds and the resilience of Caribbean coral reefs. *Nature, 450*(7166), 98-101. https://doi.org/10.1038/nature06252

National Geographic Society. (n.d.). *Tectonic plates*. National Geographic Society. https://www.nationalgeographic.org/encyclopedia/tectonic-plates/

National Park Service. (n.d.). *About Us*. National Park Service. https://www.nps.gov/aboutus/index.htm

National Park Service. (n.d.). *El Yunque National Forest*. National Park Service. https://www.nps.gov/elyu/index.htm

Paiewonsky, M. (1998). *A Brief History of the Caribbean*. Farrar, Straus and Giroux.

Pickvisa. (n.d.). *7 Things to Know Before Going to Curaçao: Travel Tips*. Pickvisa. https://pickvisa.com/blog/things-to-know-before-going-to-Curaçao

PlanetWare. (n.d.). *12 Best Resorts in Curaçao*. https://www.planetware.com/netherlands-antilles/top-rated-resorts-in-Curaçao-nan-1-2.htm

PlanetWare. (n.d.). *12 Top-Rated Tourist Attractions in the Bahamas*. PlanetWare. https://www.planetware.com/tourist-attractions/bahamas-bah.htm

Puerto Rico Herald. (2003, December 9). Puerto Rican Americans. https://www.puertorico-herald.org/issues/vol7n49

Puerto Rico Tourism Company. (n.d.). *Gastronomy*. Discover Puerto Rico. https://www.discoverpuertorico.com/gastronomy

Puerto Rico Tourism Company. (n.d.). *Things to Do*. Discover Puerto Rico. https://www.discoverpuertorico.com/things-to-do/

Puerto Rico Weather. (n.d.). *Climate Puerto Rico*. National Weather Service. https://www.weather.gov/sju/climate_puertorico

ResearchGate. (n.d.). *Geological and hydrological features of the karst system of the northern coast of Puerto Rico*. https://www.researchgate.net/publication/284887195_Geological_and_hydrological_features_of_the_karst_system_of_the_northern_coast_of_Puerto_Rico

Roatan Tourism Bureau. (n.d.). *About Roatan*. Roatan Tourism Bureau. https://roatantourismbureau.com/about-roatan/

Roatan Tourism Bureau. (n.d.). *Historical attractions*. Roatan Tourism Bureau. https://roatantourismbureau.com/what-to-do-in-roatan/historical-attractions/

Roatan Tourism Bureau. (n.d.). *Roatan Food & Drink*. Roatan Tourism Bureau. https://roatantourismbureau.com/roatan-food-drink/

Roatan Tourism Bureau. (n.d.). *Roatan island history and culture*. Roatan Tourism Bureau. https://roatantourismbureau.com/roatán-island-history-and-culture/

Rodriguez, M. (2019). The Influence of Three Cultures in Puerto Rican Food. *Néctar News*.

Saborea Puerto Rico. (n.d.). *About*. Saborea Puerto Rico. https://www.saboreapuertorico.com/about/

Sandals Resorts. (n.d.). *Sandals Blog*. Sandals.com. https://www.sandals.com/blog

Savage, J. M. (2002). *The Amphibians and Reptiles of Costa Rica: A Herpetofauna between Two Continents, between Two Seas*. University of Chicago Press.

Science Learning Hub. (n.d.). *Cretaceous period*. Science Learning Hub. https://www.sciencelearn.org.nz/resources/1831-cretaceous-period

Shantz, A. A., & Burkepile, D. E. (2014). Context-dependent effects of nutrient loading on the coral–algal mutualism. *Ecology, 95*(7), 1995-2005. https://doi.org/10.1890/13-2015.1

St. Kitts Tourism Authority. (n.d.). *Accommodations*. St. Kitts Tourism Authority. https://www.stkittstourism.kn/accommodations/

St. Kitts Tourism Authority. (n.d.). *Location*. St. Kitts Tourism Authority. https://www.stkittstourism.kn/location/

St. Kitts Tourism Authority. (n.d.). *St. Kitts*. St. Kitts Tourism Authority. https://www.stkittstourism.kn/

St. Kitts Tourism Authority. (n.d.). *St. Kitts and Nevis.* St. Kitts Tourism Authority. https://www.stkittstourism.kn/

The Broke Backpacker. (2021, January 7). *Where to Stay in Curaçao (2021 Guide): Insider Tips & Best Areas.* The Broke Backpacker. https://www.thebrokebackpacker.com/where-to-stay-in-Curaçao/

The Culture Trip. (n.d.). *15 Traditional Foods to Try in Curaçao.* The Culture Trip. https://theculturetrip.com/caribbean/Curaçao/articles/15-traditional-foods-to-try-in-Curaçao/

The Culture Trip. (n.d.). *The 10 Best Bahamas Hotels - Where to Stay in the Bahamas.* Theculturetrip.com. https://theculturetrip.com/caribbean/the-bahamas/articles/the-10-best-bahamas-hotels-where-to-stay-in-the-bahamas/

The Culture Trip. (n.d.). *The Top 10 Foods You Have to Try in Barbados.* The Culture Trip. https://theculturetrip.com/caribbean/barbados/articles/the-top-10-foods-you-have-to-try-in-barbados/

The International Ecotourism Society. (n.d.). *What is ecotourism?* The International Ecotourism Society. https://www.ecotourism.org/what-is-ecotourism/

The Islands of The Bahamas. (n.d.). *About The Bahamas.* The Islands of The Bahamas. https://www.bahamas.com/about-bahamas

The Islands of The Bahamas. (n.d.). *Climate.* The Islands of The Bahamas. https://www.bahamas.com/about-bahamas/climate

The Telegraph. (n.d.). *Barbados Travel Guide.* The Telegraph. https://www.telegraph.co.uk/travel/destinations/caribbean/barbados/

TripAdvisor. (n.d.). *Hotels in Dominica.* TripAdvisor. https://www.tripadvisor.com/Hotels-g147281-Dominica-Hotels.html

Trips To Discover. (n.d.). *10 Best All-Inclusive Resorts in the Bahamas.* Tripstodiscover.com. https://www.tripstodiscover.com/best-all-inclusive-resorts-in-the-bahamas/

U.S. Department of State. (n.d.). *Maldives - Country Information.* Travel.State.Gov. https://travel.state.gov/content/travel/en/international-travel/International-Travel-Country-Information-Pages/Maldives.html

U.S. Department of State. (n.d.). *Puerto Rico.* Travel.State.Gov. https://travel.state.gov/content/travel/en/international-travel/International-Travel-Country-Information-Pages/PuertoRico.html

U.S. Department of State. (n.d.). *The Bahamas.* U.S. Department of State. https://www.state.gov/countries-areas/the-bahamas/

U.S. Department of State. (n.d.). *The Bahamas Travel Advisory.* Travel.state.gov. https://travel.state.gov/content/travel/en/traveladvisories/traveladvisories/the-bahamas-travel-advisory.html

U.S. Embassy in Barbados, the Eastern Caribbean, and the OECS. (n.d.). *Visas.* U.S. Embassy in Barbados, the Eastern Caribbean, and the OECS. https://bb.usembassy.gov/u-s-citizen-services/local-resources-of-u-s-citizens/visas/

U.S. Embassy in Honduras. (n.d.). *Visa Requirements.* U.S. Embassy in Honduras. https://hn.usembassy.gov/visas/nonimmigrant-visas/

U.S. News & World Report. (n.d.). *Best Hotels in Curaçao.* https://travel.usnews.com/Hotels/Curaçao/

UNESCO. (n.d.). *Brimstone Hill Fortress National Park.* UNESCO. https://whc.unesco.org/en/list/910/

United Nations. (n.d.). *Dominica.* United Nations Sustainable Development Goals. https://www.un.org/sustainabledevelopment/es/country/dominica/

University of California Museum of Paleontology. (n.d.). *The Tertiary Period.* University of California Museum of Paleontology. https://ucmp.berkeley.edu/tertiary/tertiary.php

Visit Barbados. (n.d.). *Barbados Climate*. Visit Barbados. https://www.visitbarbados.org/barbados-climate

Visit Barbados. (n.d.). *Culture*. Visit Barbados. https://www.barbados.org/culture.htm

Visit Barbados. (n.d.). *Where to Stay*. Visit Barbados. https://www.visitbarbados.org/where-to-stay

Visit Jamaica. (n.d.). *Negril*. Visit Jamaica. https://www.visitjamaica.com/places-to-go/westmoreland/negril/

Visit Maldives. (n.d.). *Accommodation*. Visitmaldives.com. https://visitmaldives.com/en/accommodation/

Visit Maldives. (n.d.). *Cuisine*. Visit Maldives. https://visitmaldives.com/en/cuisine

Visit Maldives. (n.d.). *Culture and Tradition*. Visit Maldives. http://www.visitmaldives.com/en/culture-and-tradition

Visit Maldives. (n.d.). *National Parks, Reserves and Protected Areas*. Visit Maldives. https://visitmaldives.com/en/things-to-do/national-parks-reserves-and-protected-areas/

Visit Maldives. (n.d.). *Shopping*. Visit Maldives. https://visitmaldives.com/en/things-to-do/shopping

Visit St. Kitts. (n.d.). *Accommodations*. Visit St. Kitts. https://www.stkittstourism.kn/accommodations/

Visit St. Kitts. (n.d.). *Discover St. Kitts*. Visit St. Kitts. https://www.stkittstourism.kn/

Wanderlust. (n.d.). *Maldives Weather and Climate: All You Need to Know*. Wanderlust. http://www.wanderlust.co.uk/content/maldives-weather-and-climate-all-you-need-to-know/

Weather Forecast. (n.d.). *Martinique*. Weather Forecast. https://www.weather-forecast.com/locations/Martinique/forecasts/latest

Weather Forecast. (n.d.). *Puerto Rico*. Weather Forecast. https://www.weather-forecast.com/locations/Puerto-Rico/forecasts/latest

WorldAtlas. (n.d.). *Negril Island*. WorldAtlas. https://www.worldatlas.com/islands/negril-island

World Atlas. (n.d.). *Where is Martinique?* Worldatlas.com. https://www.worldatlas.com/where-is-martinique.html

World Climate Guide. (n.d.). *Saint Kitts and Nevis Climate Guide*. World Climate Guide. https://www.worldclimateguide.co.uk/climates/saint-kitts-and-nevis/

World Heritage List. (n.d.). *La Fortaleza and San Juan National Historic Site in Puerto Rico*. UNESCO World Heritage Centre. https://whc.unesco.org/en/list/910/

World Meteorological Organization. (2021, August 9). *Impactos del cambio climático en la región del Caribe: Dominica lucha por adaptarse a los riesgos crecientes*. WMO. https://public.wmo.int/es/media/comunicados-de-prensa/impactos-del-cambio-clim%C3%A1tico-en-la-reg

World Weather Online. (n.d.). *Curaçao Weather Averages*. https://www.worldweatheronline.com/Curaçao-weather-averages/Curaçao/cw.aspx

World Weather Online. (n.d.). *Martinique Weather*. World Weather Online. https://www.worldweatheronline.com/martinique-weather.aspx

World Weather Online. (n.d.). *Martinique Weather*. World Weather Online. https://www.worldweatheronline.com/martinique-weather.aspx

World Weather Online. (n.d.). *Saint Kitts and Nevis Weather*. World Weather Online. https://www.worldweatheronline.com/saint-kitts-and-nevis-weather/climate

World Wildlife Fund. (2021, December 9). *Maldives*. WWF. https://wwf.panda.org/discover/our_focus/climate_and_energy_practice/ndcs_we_want/reviewed_ndcs_/maldives/

WWF. (n.d.). *NT0212 - Venezuelan Coastal Range.* World Wildlife Fund. https://www.worldwildlife.org/ecoregions/nt0212

Zimmermann, K. A. (2019, October 3). *Barbados.* Encyclopedia Britannica. https://www.britannica.com/place/Barbados

Zimmermann, K. A. (n.d.). *History of Barbados.* Visit Barbados. https://www.visitbarbados.org/about-barbados/history-of-barbados

Printed in Great Britain
by Amazon

26019709R00073